Jürgen Seefeldt and Ludger Syré

Portals to the Past and to the Future –
Libraries in Germany

Jürgen Seefeldt and Ludger Syré

Portals to the Past and to the Future – Libraries in Germany

Published by the Bundesvereinigung Deutscher Bibliotheksverbände e.V.
(Federal Union of German Library Associations)

With an Introductory Essay and an Epilogue by Georg Ruppelt

Translated by Diann Rusch-Feja

2003
Georg Olms Verlag
Hildesheim ·Zürich · New York

Bibliografische Information Der Deutschen Bibliothek
Die Deutsche Bibliothek verzeichnet diese Publikation
in der deutschen Nationalbibliografie; detaillierte bibliografische Daten
sind im Internet über *http://dnb.ddb.de* abrufbar.

Bibliographic information published by Die Deutsche Bibliothek
Die Deutsche Bibliothek lists this publication in the
Deutsche Nationalbibliografie; detailed bibliographic data are
available in the Internet at *http://dnb.ddb.de*.

♾ ISO 9706
© Georg Olms Verlag, Hildesheim 2003
www.olms.de
Alle Rechte vorbehalten
Printed in Germany
Gedruckt auf säurefreiem, alterungsbeständigem Papier
Umschlagentwurf: Barbara Gutjahr
Gestaltung: Franziska Land
Herstellung: Druckhaus Köthen GmbH
ISBN 3-487-11713-4

Table of Contents

CRISIS AND AWAKENING
GERMAN LIBRARIANSHIP AT THE BEGINNING
OF THE 21ST CENTURY

An Introduction

Georg Ruppelt

This is indeed a wonderful image: the library as a door, a gate, a portal! A wealth of associations appear with this mental picture. The image of the portal could mean access to knowledge, to information, to science, to culture and to education. When harbor cities designate themselves as the gateways to the world, this has always meant globality. In principle, libraries today are available world-wide to everyone, as long as the necessary means and skills are present. They are gate(way)s to the world of unlimited information.

An open door invites one to enter. In Germany, the doors of the libraries are opened for people of all ages and social classes, totally independent of their level of education or country of origin. Thus, it is an especially suitable motto which the IFLA (*International Federation of Library Associations and Institutions*) has chosen for its World Conference in 2003 in Berlin: The library as a portal. This image also awakens an association to the emblem of the German capital city, the Brandenburg Gate. Even the Federation of German Library Associations (*Bundesvereinigung Deutscher Bibliotheksverbände*, abbreviated "*BDB*") has used this image as the title of this present book and thereby consciously established the temporal connection: the gate as a metaphor for the present through which one steps from the past into the future.

In ancient Rome, the two-faced head of the god of entrance was frequently found on doors, gates and passage ways: Janus' two faces presented on one side a friendly and the other side an unfriendly face. Janus symbolizes the spatial as well as the temporal passage, namely, the passage from the past into the future. The past, as well as the present, of German librarianship can, in turn, favourably illuminate the visage of the observer in the year 2003, or cast it into shadowed distress. We would like to look back for a moment decade by decade to illustrate some of the events, and in-

vestigate these in their relationships to our current situation.

In the 20th century, we first confront an event in 1913 which serves our purpose, namely, the opening of the *Deutsche Bücherei* in Leipzig, which had been founded the year before. It should be emphasized that the *Deutsche Bücherei* was founded on the initiative of the Association of the German Book Trade (*Börsenverein für den deutschen Buchhandel*) – not by the German government! While in other European countries national libraries had already stood at the center of that country's librarianship for decades or even centuries, in Germany it was only in the 20th century that a central institution for librarianship which collected the entire book production of the country was founded. If one considers that the *Deutsche Bücherei* began its collection activities only 40 years after the establishment of the German Empire (*Deutsches Reich*) while, for example, the German Museum of Masterpieces in the Natural Sciences and Technology (*Deutsches Museum von Meisterwerken der Naturwissenschaft und Technik*) in Munich had already been established 10 years earlier in 1903, then one cannot avoid having the impression that the cultivation of central library functions was not a focal point of importance in the scientific and educational policies of the German state governments. Thus, a certain continuity in German history is evident, despite the violent upheavals of the last 100 years.

The traditional independence of the German Federal states (*Länder*) in the areas of culture and education has certainly produced a multitude of cultural monuments, to which libraries also belong, more than are known in any other centrally governed countries. In his 1947 novel *Dr. Faustus,* Thomas Mann noted the German emphasis and esteem of regional, even local culture in his description of the ficticious city "Kaisersaschern": "[...]but Kaiseraschern, a central train hub, is, with its 27,000 inhabitants, definitely self-sufficient and feels itself, as every German city, to be a cultural center of historical instrinsic worth. It derives its sustinence from various industries [...] and possesses in addition to its museum of cultural history – which boasts of a chamber with crass torture instruments- a very valuable library of 25,000 volumes and 5000 manuscripts [...]."

As much as one values and admires today the variety created by the cultural independence of the regions or the cultural and educational autonomy of the German Federal States today, however, in the face of financial crises, it can also be seen how difficult it is to develop or to establish and maintain the necessary key institutions for librarianship. If political irrationality is combined with these structural problems, then such decisions are made as those made at the end of the 20th century which destined the German Library Institute (*Deutsches Bibliotheksinstitut – DBI*), founded at the beginning of the 1970's, to liquidation. Arguments about the cultural and educational autonomy of the *Länder* in a so-called "decentralization debate" on the one hand, and political irrationality in our immediate present on the other hand have led to the circumstances that a small, but highly effective successor institution, the Innovation Center for Libraries (*Innovationszentrum für Bibliotheken – IZB*), although meticulously planned in every detail, could not be established. The result of this development is that a country-wide planning and service center for libraries is no longer possible at the beginning of the 21st century, and all that remains for those library associations which are united in the *Bundesvereinigung Deutscher Bibliotheksverbände* and who protested loudly, but unsuccessfully in preventing the dissolution – yes, even abortion – of central institutions, is now the tedious task of attempting to at least salvage the marginal remnants and shattered remains of a central library service center or to establish it anew.

Ten years after the opening of the *Deutsche Bücherei* in Leipzig and after a World War had been lost, academic and research libraries in Germany were confronted with an existential crisis in 1923 as a result of the exorbitant inflation. The normal means for acquisitions, especially for foreign literature, were simply not available, and many academic and research libraries were happy that they could turn the duplicates from their collections into cash or exchange them. According to the Treaty of Versaille, Germany had to give these up for the reconstruction of the University Library of Louvain which had been destroyed by the artillery bombardment.

In these euphemistically named "financially weak" years after the First World War, the "Emergency Council of German Science" (*Notgemeinschaft der deutschen Wissenschaft*), which later named itself "The German Council for the Preservation and Advancement of Research" (*Deutsche Gemeinschaft zur Erhaltung und Förderung der Forschung*), in abbreviated form, "Research Council", was founded. The "German Research Council" (*Deutsche Forschungsgemeinschaft – DFG*), as it has been called since the Second World War, has graciously provided the German libraries with quantitatively as well as qualitatively highly valuable and comprehensive acquisition support continuing up to the present time. This support includes, among other programs, the national "Special Subject Collection Area Program" (*Sondersammelgebietsprogramm*).

This program was only possible through the close cooperation of libraries across and beyond the *Länder* borders. It can be deemed as the positive result of the federalistic structure in Germany that libraries and also librarian organisations showed a decisive commitment to cooperation and networking. Take, for instance, the successful model of interlibrary loan with which the library computer networks were established, or even the creation of the *Bundesvereinigung Deutscher Bibliotheksverbände*, which, since the beginning of the 21st century, in addition to the library organizations, has united the *Goethe Institute – Inter Nationes*, the *Bertelsmann Foundation*, and the *ekz-Library Service GmbH* under its auspices. Especially in German librarianship, because of its federal structure (excluding the non-democratic times), the *Bundesvereinigung Deutscher Bibliotheksverbände* has shown how successfully libraries can work together for their interests and the interests of their clientele.

Connected to this aspect, we must point out the project *Bibliothek 2007* which was initiated by the BDB and the Bertelsmann Foundation. The focus of this project is to work out a recommendation for the future design of librarianship in Germany which should stimulate both the professional and political discussion on opportunities for optimizing the structures and performance of libraries and will initiate a overlapping strategic process at the Federal level, at the *Länder* level and at the municipal level. The first results are expected in the year 2003 – unfortunately only after the printing of this book.

However, while the friendly Janus face looks at the cooperation between German libraries and library organizations, at the same time the viewer looking backwards is much more inclined to turn his face away from the atrocious events of the twelve years after 1933. Of course, this is precisely what we cannot do, rather we must confront our past. The 10th of May, 1933, the day on which books from German public libraries were burned, will always belong to the most ignominious dates of German librarianship. Historical research has worked through in detail and has come to terms with the processes of "purging" and "enforced conformity" of the libraries. However, there is a chapter of this story which has only succeeded in slightly penetrating the public awareness – even the awareness of the library public. What is meant here, are the library possessions which, as a result of the confiscation or theft of the possessions of Jewish citizens or politically persecuted persons, landed on the storage shelves of our libraries. With the exception of the example of a few libraries and individual research projects, even at the beginning of the 21st century, exhaustive investigations are still shamefully missing, and because of that, also the corresponding restitution.

In view of this background, the State Library of Lower Saxony together with the State Parliament (*Landtag*) of Lower Saxony conducted a symposium with the theme "Jewish Book Possession as Spoils of War" which took place in November 2002 and found international acclaim. As a result of the symposium, the "Hanover Appeal" (*Hannoversche Appell*) urged that these stolen goods be searched for systematically in German libraries, that the evidence and knowledge be made public, and that the identified collections be returned to the rightful heirs of those from whom they had been stolen. Furthermore, the Hanover Appeal recommended that librarian training institutions reinstate library history, especially that of the time of National Socialism, in their curricula.

The reference in the Hanover Appeal to this Desiderata in librarian training stands in direct connection with a topic which has been discussed in Germany for the last several years with vehemence. The question discussed is whether it makes sense to continue to stock libraries with conventional media, that is to say, books and journals, or to shift completely to electronic media. The discussion also touches on – in a certain way – a phenomena which Ray Bradbury had described in a visionary way 50 years ago in his novel *Fahrenheit 451*. In 1953, Bradbury portrayed a society in which books were forbidden and burned (Fahrenheit 451 is 223 degrees Celsius, the temperature at which paper spontaneously burns), and in which book owners and readers of books were persecuted. The people in this country were informed and entertained exclusively through television and electronic media. Thus, in Bradbury's novel, a mass society, in which the word "individualism" had become an invective, evolved without political coercion.

Now at the beginning of the 21st century, German democracy has no resemblance at all to the kind of society described by Ray Bradbury in his novel. But some things still do indicate that fascination, as well as the necessity, with electronic communication has led to the situation that libraries and their organisations are in danger of neglecting their own past, and connected with that the immense number of intellectual jewels for which they are responsible. A certain disrespect or even considerable disinterest towards the collections of books belonging to the pre-digital era seems to have spread itself over many areas. This, in turn, could lead to the situation in Germany that not enough media specialists will be trained who will be able to recover these historical intellectual treasures.

50 years after the publication of *Fahrenheit 451*, the blatant weaknesses of the German educational and training system are evident. International and national studies have confirmed that the youth in our larger industrial nations have, for the most part, an unsatisfactory level of education; hence, the data on reading competencies are shocking. The *Bundesvereinigung Deutscher Bibliotheksverbände*, the "Foundation for Reading" (*Stiftung Lesen*) and for that reason, many other political, cultural and societal groups insist on comprehensive educational reforms. In addition to that is the fact that libraries must be supported to a greater degree despite – or precisely because of – the financial crisis in public funding. The promotion of reading is still an essential task for our libraries, especially in view of the fact that media competen-

cies can only be attained based on a solid foundation in the cultural technique of reading.

Thirty years ago, the situation in major parts of Germany was still characterized by great optimism and the sense that a new era was about to dawn. In the *Bibliotheksplan '73,* future-oriented standards for information provision and stocking of public, as well as academic and research libraries, were established, and the appeal for stronger cooperation between the various sections of librarianship was made. Even if the standards set were only rarely achieved and only as an example in the municipalities during the following years, nevertheless, public libraries could still be developed considerably. In the area of academic and research libraries, a significant number of new libraries were established at the higher education institutions.

German libraries, as well as the bodies representing them, can look back with pride and satisfaction on two achievements in the past 30 years. The reunification of Germany at the beginning of the 1990's with respect to libraries was carried out highly effectively, rapidly and pleasantly "soundless." What might have contributed to this was the fact that German librarians of both parts of Germany had maintained contact among themselves – at the professional and even at the collegial level – in the decades before, despite political and physical barriers, so that it had never completely been lost. A considerable contribution to this "growing together" was made by the associations which had united under the umbrella of the *Bundesvereinigung Deutscher Bibliotheksverbände.*

A first, and on the whole, a very positive stocktaking of librarianship in unified Germany, was able to be presented by the *BDB* 10 years ago with the book, *Bibliotheken '93. Strukturen, Aufgaben, Positionen,* which is indispensable – even today. In this book, the situation of German librarianship on the eve of the turn of the century is described en gros and en detail. The development of electronic data processing and an international network are not only called for in academic and research libraries, but also in public libraries. And with that we have named the second area in which German libraries have made great advances over the last 10 years.

Today, academic and research libraries, as well as public libraries, in Germany are a component of the global digital information society and are judged favorably in international comparison. While the charge of *Bibliotheken '93* that Germany should take on a leading role in the production and use of electronic media and networks, has essentially been met – even if this is an on-going charge – one might have considerable hesitation about the depth of fulfilment of other points from this list of demands from 1993; unfortunately, they have not become irrelevant:

"The public library does not belong to the obligations of the municipalities – therefore in times of austerity their budgets will be cut first. In the universities, the deficits in the library literature offerings are growing at a horrifying rate, while at the same time the means for acquisitions are stagnating, while book and even more so journal prices, as well as the additional need for electronic media, are rising. Still, libraries and their services were never so much in demand and so urgently needed as today. This is because it will be decisive for our future

· that children and youth learn to master the cultural technique of reading despite the constant bombardment from television;

· that the variety of opinions in the broad representative selection for everyone in libraries remains freely accessible;

· that school pupils and students, workers and independent businessmen, teachers and researchers can rapidly receive and use subject-oriented and scientific literature with sufficient numbers of copies in their areas of interest and even for the most specific topics."

The fact that the difficulties of German libraries at present are openly discussed in this introductory essay, shows that the problems are recognized – which is the first requirement for solving them. In this, it is undoubtedly proven that Germany is blessed with a highly effective and well-functioning library network. The historical and modern intellectual treasures present in Germany's libraries are worth being cataloged and presented to the world. With its public libraries, Germany can contribute to education and to the coexistence of diverse cultures. This is most likely also one of the reasons for IFLA to hold its conference in the year 2003 in Berlin. For librarians in reunited Germany, it is a great honor and source of joy to host the IFLA 2003. We hope that impulses will radiate from this conference which will stimulate librarians to greater international cooperation and strengthen cultural understanding for peace, collegiality, and perhaps even friendship.

Translation of German Diagrams

Note to the reader: Because it was not possible to translate the graphs and diagrams directly into the diagrams for printing this book, the editorial board decided to print the German maps and diagrams in the English translation with a legend to these diagrams here. The left column is the German text corresponding top-down to the diagram and the right side below is the English translation most appropriate to the term as used in the graph or diagram. The diagrams are given here in order as they appear with the page number in parentheses after the title of the diagram.

Administrative Structure of a *Bundesland (Land)* (p.26)

Landesparlament	State / *Land* Parliament
Landesregierung	State / *Land* Government
Innenministerium	Ministry of the Interior
Justizministerium	Minsitry of Justice
Kultusministerium	Ministry of Culture
Finanzministerium	Ministry of Finance
Wirtschaftsministerium	Ministry of Economics
Regierungspräsidenten	The Governing Presidents (of each *Land*)
Bezirksregierung	District Government
Landkreis	County
Städte und Gemeinden	Cities and Communities (Townships)

The Fundamental Elements of the Three-Tiered School System in Germany (p.28)

hauptsächliche handwerkliche Ausbildungsberufe = primarily craftsman professions
(fast) alle Ausbildungsberufe = (almost all professions with apprenticeships)
Alle Ausbildungsberufe / Zugang zu Universitäten = All professions with apprenticeships / Entrance Requirements to the Universities
Hauptschulabschluss = Lower High School Degree (Hauptschule)
Realschulabschluss = Lower High School Degree (Realschule)
Abitur / Allgemeine Hochschulreife = Abitur Degree / General Requirements for Entrance to Tertial Educational Institutions
Jahre = Years
Hauptschule = Lower High School / Middle School (Hauptschule)
Realschule = Lower High School / Middle School (Realschule)
Gymnasium = Gymnasium (College Preparatory Track, Upper High School)
Grundschule = Elementary School
4 Jahre, Pflicht für alle Schüler = 4 years, mandatory for all pupils

Organization of an Expanded Metropolitan Library System (p. 53)

Zentralbibliothek / Hauptstelle	Central library / Main library
Kinder- und Jugendbibliothek	Children's and Youth Library
Artothek	Art Collection
Bezirksbibliothek / Stadtteilbibliothek	District or Borough Library
Musikbibliothek	Music Library
Zweigbibliotheken	Branch Libraries
Mediothek	Media Center
Schulbibliothek	School Library
Fahrbibliothek	Mobile Library
Patientenbibliothek	Patients' Library at a Hospital

Professions in Public and Academic/Research Libraries (Public Service) – Overview of Career Levels (p. 64)

Functional Description Employee	Official Designation Civil Servant	Salary Group / Wage Bracket
Director of City Library	Head Director of City Library	BAT I / Wage Br. A 1
Director of City Library	City Library Director	BAT Ia / Wage Br. A 15
Director of City Library Deputy Director	Senior Library Official	BAT Ib / Wage Br. A 14
Director of City Library Deputy Director Departmental Head	Library Official Senior Official (after retirement)	BAT IIa / Wage Br. A 13
Director of City Library Deputy Director Departmental Head	Library Senior Official	BAT III / Wage Br. A 12
Head of the City Library Deputy Head Departmental Head	Senior Librarian	BAT IVa / Wage Br. A 11
Head of City Library Deputy Head Branch Director	Certified Librarian Certified Official	BAT IVb / Wage Br. A 10
Head of City Library Deputy Head Branch Director	Certified Librarian Certified Official	BAT Vb / Wage Br. A 9
Library Assistant Skilled Employee	Library Assistant	BAT VI / Wage Br. A 8
Library Assistant Skilled Lib. Employee	Library Assistant Official	BAT VII / Wage Br. A 7
Library Assistant Skilled Employee	Library Secretary	BAT VIII – VII Wage Br. A 6 / A 5

Division of Library Professions with Selected Activities Using the Example of a Metropolitan Library (p.65)

Examples for Activities in Comparison

University Study
Senior Service / Subject Librarians
1. Information on Collections and Electronic Resources
Reference and Advice on Scholarly Questions
2. Public Relations & Promotion
Scholarly Exhibitions, Planning and Coordination of Cultural Management
3. Collection Development and Acquisitions
Creation of Collection Development Guidelines
Content Responsibility for Collection Development
Subject Literature Review, Responsibility for Acquisitions Budget

Study at University of Applied Science
Upper Service
1. Information on Collections and Electronic Resources
Searching in Reference Works, Databases and Networked Information
2. Public Relations & Promotion
Hold Lectures, Organize Bibliographic Services
3. Collection Development and Acquisitions
Coordination of Collection Development, Negotiation of Delivery Conditions and Agreements

Professional Vocational Training
Skilled (Middle) Service
1. Information on Collections and Electronic Resources
Collaboration in Preparing Guides, Information on Locating Items
2. Public Relations & Promotion
Conduct Staff Training and Class Tours
3. Collection Development and Acquisitions
Accession, Processing and Invoice Processing
Prepare and Monitor Budgetary Lists & Expenditures

On-the-Job Training
Unskilled Service
1. Information on Collections and Electronic Resources
Circulation Activities, Sending Photocopies (for Interlibrary Loan)
2. Public Relations & Promotion
Print, Copy & Send Promotional Materials
3. Collection Development and Acquisitions
Collect Statistics, Receive Deliveries, Correspondence, Orders, Running Errands

Members of the Federation of German Library Associations (p. 69)

(This diagram shows the association members of the Bundesvereinigung Deutscher Bibliotheksverbände e.V. (BDB)). The English translation of the association names can be found in the corresponding text sections, so this diagram should be able to be interpreted with additional translation here.)

DBV – German Libraries Association (p. 70)

The Association Bodies and Divisions of the DBV in Sections and Regional Branches (*Landesverbände*)

Executive: 1 President, 2 Vice-Presidents, Council, Executive Board, 1 Chair, 6 Substitutes, ad hoc groups of experts

Sections: Regional Branches / State Associations: Section 1. Public Libraries for cities with over 400,000 inhabitants, Section 2. Public Libraries for cities with 300,000–400,000 inhabitants, Section 3a. Public Libraries for cities with 50,000–300,000 inhabitants, Section 3b. Public Libraries for cities of up to 50,000 inhabitants, Section 4. Scholarly Universal Libraries, Section 5. Scholarly Special Libraries, Section 6. Supraregional and regional institutions for librarianship (state and ecclesiastical library service centers), Section 7. Librarian Training Institutions (Universities, Universities of Applied Science, Library Schools), Section 8. Public Libraries in Corporations, Patient Libraries in Hospitals, Prison Libraries

15 Regional Branches / State Associations: Baden-Württemberg, Bavaria, Berlin-Brandenburg, Bremen, Hamburg, Hesse, Lower Saxony, North Rhine-Westphalia, Rhineland-Palatinate, the Saarland, Saxony, Saxony-Anhalt, Schleswig-Holstein, Thuringia
General Assembly (of members)

Structure of the German Libraries Association (BIB) (p. 72)

Jährliche Mitgliederver-sammlung	Annual General Assembly
Vorstand	Executive Board
1 Vorsitz., 4 Stellvertreter	1 Chair, 4 Representatives
Amtsperiode: 3 Jahre	Term of Office: 3 years
15 Landesgruppen	15 State Groups
3-5 köpfiger Vorstand	(3-5 person board)
5 Kommissionen	5 Commissions
3–5 Mitglieder	(3–5 members)
1 beruf. Hrsg.	1 professional editor
Baden-Württemberg ...	[names of the Länder]
Komm. Aus- und Fortbildung	Commission for Training and Continuing Professional Development
Komm. Eingruppierung u. Besoldung	Commission for Employment Status & Wage Levels
Komm. Neue Technologien	Commission for New Technologies
Komm. Eine-Person-Bibliotheken	Commission for One Person Libraries
Komm. von Informationen von Fachangestellten und Assistenten	Commission on Information for Skilled Employees and Library Assistants
2 gewählte Hrsg.	2 elected / editors
3 fest angestellte Redakteure	3 permanent editors
3 Herausgeber	3 Editors
10 köpf. Redaktionsbeirat	10 person editorial board

(p. 67)
Librarian Training Institutions in Germany

		Degrees Awarded:
Berlin:	Humboldt University of Berlin Institute for Library Science	Academic/Research Librarian Magister Atrium (MA) Doctorate
Darmstadt:	University of Applied Science: Department Information and Knowledge Management	Certified Information Broker (equivalent to Certified Librarian)
Hamburg:	University for Applied Sciences Hamburg: Department Library and Information	Certified Librarian Certified Documentalist (Media Specialist)
Hanover:	University of Applied Science Hanover: Course of Study Information Management	Certified Librarian Certified Information Broker
Coblence: Landau:	University of Coblence / Landau: Distance Learning: Library and Information Science (in cooperation with the Humboldt University Berlin)	Magister Artium (MA)
Cologne:	University of Applied Science Cologne: Department of Information and Communication Science	Certified Librarian Certified Information Broker Master of Library and Information Science
Leipzig:	University for Technology, Economics and Culture: Department of Book and Museum	Certified Librarian
Munich:	Bavarian Administrative Academy Munich (BSB): Department of Archives and Librarianship	Certified Librarian (at Academic and Research Libraries) Senior Librarian
Potsdam:	University of Applied Science Potsdam: Department of Information Sciences Certified Documentalist Academic Documentalist	Certified Librarian Certified Archivist
Stuttgart:	University of Applied Science Stuttgart – Media Academie (HdM), Department of Information and Communication	Certified Librarian Certified Information Broker Bachelor / Master of Information and Communication

1 HISTORY

Lines of Development of German Library History

For anyone who would like to understand the structure and current situation of German librarianship, a short excursion into German history is absolutely essential. A look at the historical map of Germany in the various epochs provides two important pieces of information:

· The central European area, which unified those groups of people using the Germanic vernacular, shows various territorial dimensions during the centuries. Despite constantly changing borders, at the latest by the end of the first millennium, the "German Empire" had been formed.

· During this period, what was the later "German Empire" had always been divided into individual territories whose number could only be determined with difficulty in the earliest centuries. However, by 1803 (or more exactly 1815) this number had shrunken considerably. The division according to states after the founding of the "German Empire" in 1871 continued, and up to today this has determined the structure of the Federal Republic of Germany, which since 1949 is a federated country with 16 "Länder" (states).

Since Germany was never a centralized state, the cultural life developed and unfolded primarily in the individual territories and states, and therefore assumed a distinct regional character. The Basic Law (Grundgesetz) and the Constitution of the Federal Republic of Germany refer back to this historical tradition when it defers the responsibility for almost all cultural matters of importance to the competencies of the Länder. This explains to a great extent why even librarianship developed at the regional level, has retained its character, and up to the present has been determined by the primarily decentralized structure.

The *Library of the Hildesheim Cathedral* (Lower Saxony), which traces its beginnings to the founding of the Diocese 815, possesses a Book of Hours which was written in the second half of the 15th Century in Latin and French, and which evidences a unique form: the 266 parchment pages of the *Codex Rotundus* (HS 728) have been cut to a circle with the diameter of 9 cm.

From the Middle Ages up to Secularization

Even if libraries may have already existed in the larger cities of the Roman province of Germania, the history of German librarianship does not begin in antiquity but rather in the Middle Ages. Spreading out from Italy and Spain, monasteries developed in the 6th century A.D. to be the first sites of the culture of the book by virtue of their establishment of libraries (*armarium*) and copying rooms (*scriptorium*). Through these, the monasteries became transmitters of the classical traditions.

The first *cathedral libraries* on German soil were founded in the Carolingian period under the influence of the Irish and Anglo-Saxon missionaries in the 9th and 10th centuries (for instance, in Cologne, Mainz, Würzburg, Freising) and the *monastic libraries* (*Klosterbibliotheken*), among which Fulda, Lorsch, St. Gallen, Reichenau and Murbach were the largest, possessing several hundred volumes. By the end of the Middle Ages, the number of monastic libraries had multiplied considerably, primarily through the foundation of the new Orders (Cistercian, Augustinian Canons, Premonstratensian). Those of the mendicants who chose to live in the cities (the Dominicans and the Franciscans) dedicated themselves especially to science and tea-

ching, and therefore considered libraries to be indispensable instruments for their work.

In addition to the previous financiers of scientific activities, school communities became new locations for transfer and teaching as of the high Middle Ages (900 – 1300); with time, they joined together to form independent institutions of the *universitas magistrorum et scholarium* and formed the seeds of today's universities. In contrast to the founding of universities in Italy (Salerno, Bologna), France (Paris), Spain (Salamanca) and England (Oxford), Germany's first universities were founded some 150 years later. However, this led to the creation of new collections of books – though still

The Gospel Book of Henry the Lion (*Evangeliar Heinrichs des Löwen*) was written about 1188 in the monastery Helmarshausen. Commissioned by the Guelphic Duke, it is considered as one of the most magnificent accomplishments of medieval book art. The parchment manuscript (*Cod. Guelf. 105 Noviss. 2°, illus. Fol. 19r*) is kept in the *Herzog August Library* (*Herzog August Bibliothek*) in Wolfenbüttel (Lower Saxony) and has four owners (the state of Lower Saxony, the state of Bavaria, the Federal Republic of Germany, the Prussian Cultural Heritage Foundation).

modest since the professors kept the most important works in their private libraries and students either copied the texts of their professors or wrote copious notes from their lectures. The oldest university founded in the "German Empire" of that time was in Prague (1348). That was followed by universities established in Vienna (1365), Heidelberg (1386), Cologne (1388) and Erfurt (1392).

Characteristic for the development of the book culture since the late Classical era is the transition from the scroll to the book (Codex), and the use of parchment as the replacement for papyrus for writing, later replaced by cheaper paper. Books were stored in cabinets, later in niches and on long lecterns; the enlargement of the book collection was achieved by copying and subsequent illustration of the manuscripts, and a last characteristic aspect was the dominance of the Latin language.

Because education was firmly in the hands of the clergy during the Middle Ages, books were only very rarely in the possession of laypersons. Emperor Charlemagne (742 – 814) owned a remarkable courtly library which, however, was not blessed with continuity. Many of the post-Carolingian rulers were content with presenting magnificently decorated manuscripts as gifts to monasteries and cathedrals. Only once the value of education became apparent for the nobility did the knowledge of writing and scholarship take hold, and collections of books could be found in the kings' courts, as well as in the aristocratic manors of the nobility.

Since the 13th century, the culture of writing also gained acceptance in the cities, but the number of private libraries belonging to commoners remained small and only in the Humanistic period experienced its first flowering with the library type of the *scholars' library* (*Gelehrtenbibliothek*). The *councilors' libraries* (*Ratsbüchereien*), which served the municipal administration, formed a new type of library as of the 14th century and also founded the basis for many of the later scholarly city libraries. An especially early example of this is the *Ratsbibliothek* of Nuremberg which is first referred to in the year 1370.

With the discovery of printing by Johannes Gutenberg in the middle of the 15th century and the previous transition from parchment to paper as the major writing material approximately one hundred years earlier, the basis was set for the wider, more rapid growth of library collections. The rapid

The *Schedelsche Weltchronik*, printed in 1493 by Anton Koberger in Nuremberg, with its 1,809 wood cuts (colored in after printing), belongs to the most illustrated works from the period of early imprints. Its author, the Nuremberg doctor and Humanist Dr. Hartmann Schedel, owned the largest private library of that city in his time. The illustration shows the copy owned by the *Fürstlich Hohenzollernsche Hofbibliothek in Sigmaringen* (Baden-Württemberg).

and forceful spread of printing gave flight to the spread of the premises of the Reformation, which in turn, resulted in the rise of many libraries in schools, churches and in the cities. On the other hand, the Reformation also led to the demise of the monastic libraries in wide areas of Germany because of the dissolution of many monasteries and also to the destruction of certain literature of medieval theology considered as "useless."

The Counter Reformation led to a wave of newly established libraries; in this case, it was primarily the Jesuits who required libraries for their theological colleges, and apparently the Jesuit Order was the first order which accomplished the transition from the *lectern library* (*Pultbibliothek*) to the *hall library* (*Saalbibliothek*). The ecclesiastical division continued in the universities; examples of Protestant universities are found in Marburg (1527) and Gießen (1607), and of Catholic universities in Dillingen (1551), and Würzburg (1582). The libraries of the German universities remained, admittedly, in a rather desolate condition. The number of students rose and fell greatly, but never – until the end of the 18th century – rose above the number of 4,500 students within the "German Empire."

The 15th and 16th centuries also mark the beginnings of the first *court libraries* (*Hofbibliotheken*) which partially go back to the Humanistic educational efforts and partially to the princes' needs for social status, and their development remained closely connected to the bibliophilic tendency and personal interests of the ruler himself. In addition to the Emperor's Court Library in Vienna (officialy founed in 1368), the court libraries in Munich (founded in 1558) and in Dresden (founded ca. 1556) should be noted, as well as the collections of the Heidelberg Electors which were combined in 1558 to become the *Library of the Palatinate* (*Bibliotheca Palatina*), the most well-known German library at that time.

The gold binding around the *Berthold Missale* (*Cod. bibl.* 4° 32), owned by the *Württembergische Landesbibliothek* in Stuttgart (Baden-Württemberg), was made in the second quarter of the 12th century, presumably in a Komburg workshop. The portrayal of Christ on the throne can be traced to Byzantine examples which have spread primariy through the type of book illustration practiced in the Monastery of Reichenau at Lake Constance.

15

The Library of the Benedictine Monastery of Ottobeuren (*Bibliothek des Benediktinerklosters Ottobeuren*) in the Bavarian precinct Allgäu is an excellent example of the Baroque "hall library."
Bookshelves are arranged around the entire room and continue upwards in the gallery which is built upon 44 columns of marble pieces. In the middle of the hall is the statue of the Greek goddess Pallas Athena as the protector of the sciences.

After the decline during the period of the Thirty Years' War (1618 – 1648), it was not until the 18th century that an upswing in the library construction patterned after the foreign model took place. Decoratively furnished Baroque *hall libraries,* which were installed in both monasteries and castles, reflected tendencies to follow partially practical needs, partially aesthetic aspects. As a result of the rising book production, *library catalogs* increased in significance.

Characteristic for the 17th and 18th centuries, however, was the increase of the *court libraries* (*Hofbibliotheken*), which were created by almost all German princes and rulers at that time. One of the most important princely collections was established in the small city of Wolfenbüttel, seat of the court of the Duchy of Brunswick-Lüneburg. The Elector's court library in Berlin, founded in 1661, developed into the most important German library up into the period before the Second World War; today it is the State Library of Berlin – Prussian Cultural Heritage (*Staatsbibliothek zu Berlin – Preußischer Kulturbesitz*).

Since the era of Humanism, the number of *private libraries* (*Privatbibliotheken*) belonging to writers and scholars increased precipitously. The most significant newly founded university in the period of the Enlightenment was at the University of Göttingen (1737). Because the University Library of Göttingen was established as a service unit for re-

In 1914, the Royal Library in Berlin (*Königliche Bibliothek zu Berlin*), located on the boulevard Unter den Linden, received a new building in Wilhelmine style (architect: Ernst von Ihne) which also housed the Royal Academy of the Sciences and the University Library. The showcase of this building was the round cupola hall. This photograph shows one of the eight inner courtyards with a side entrance.

search, this library pursued a carefully selective acquisition program and gave the newest publications needed by the researchers greatest priority. The books in this library were arranged roughly by a rather broad classification scheme according to subject areas. The first Reform university, the University in Halle, was opened in 1694 and soon had a higher number of students than any other German higher education institution.

The largest redistribution of book collections in history resulted from the secularization carried out in the year 1803. This took place in south and western Germany according to the same procedure that had been executed by the Protestant rulers in the other parts of Germany as a result of the Reformation. From what followed, this secularization meant a broadly planned expropriation of church possessions and transfer to the ruling governors. The book collections of the dissolved monasteries were integrated into the state libraries, predominately in the *court libraries* (*Hofbibliotheken*) and *university libraries* (*Universitätsbibliotheken*).

From the 19th Century to the Second World War

The Napoleonic era at the beginning of the 19th century put an end to many of the small states in Germany, as well as to many smaller universities that were not able to survive. Exemplary for the new university landscape was Prussia, where higher education was reformed as a result of far-reaching state reforms, and the idea of *the modern lending library* (*Gebrauchsbibliothek*) which influenced the development of the *academic library* in the 19th century took hold.

A fundamental reform of German librarianship spread after having started in Prussia in 1871. At that time, an active building period began. Stacks became the predominate form of storage for the increasingly more rapidly growing numbers of books (blossoming of all the sciences, evolution of new branches of science). Opening times were extended, lending regulations were made more liberal. In order to make the collections of all the libraries of the institutions of higher education in a particular city available to the users, initiatives for cooperation and coordination were enacted: in connection with this, the Prussian Union Catalog (*Preußischer Gesamtkatalog*), the Berlin Titles of

Printed Books (*Berliner Titeldrucke*), the Prussian Cataloguing Rules for the Alphabetical Catalog (*Preußische Instruktionen für die alphabetischen Kataloge – PI*), as well as the reference office (*Auskunftsbüro*) and the external library loan (*auswärtiger Leihverkehr*) evolved.

The rapid rise in the production of literature forced libraries to base their acquisitions policy on a more disciplined selection and led later to the establishment of collection areas of emphasis and cooperative use of collections within the framework of library loan. Furthermore, the rise in the number of copies printed – thanks to the technical advances in paper and book production (invention of the fast press, use of paper containing wood) and the consequential reduction in book prices since

The State Library in Bamberg (*Staatsbibliothek Bamberg*) (Bavaria) owes its founding in 1803 to the necessity of combining the book collections of the secularized monastery and ecclesiastic foundation of the former Bishopdom of Bamberg with the library of the university which was also abolished. Since 1965, this Library has been located in the former royal "New Residence" of the Bishop with its Baroque display room; this photo shows the Carlsberg Library located in the so-called Dominican shelves. Since 1972, Bamberg is again the home of a university.

approximately 1840, have all had a persistent effect on libraries.

Since the middle of the 19th century, the continually increasing differentiation of the disciplines at the universities led to establishing individual subject collections needed for quick reference, which in the course of time grew to become independent *faculty and departmental libraries* (*Institutsbibliotheken*) in addition to the *central university library* (*Zentralbibliothek*). The specialization of research and the rising number of publications also led to the growth of a new type of library both within and outside of the university, namely, the *special library* (*Spezialbibliothek*); thus, the times in which all libraries at least attempted to offer universal collections were gone. For the most promising area of the future in the 19th century, namely technology, individual technical universities with corresponding specially designed libraries for these needs developed (for instance, in Aachen, Berlin-Charlottenburg, Dresden, and Karlsruhe). In addition to the government, companies, clubs, societies and associations created some very important special collections in almost all areas of societal and economic aspects of life.

Characteristic of the future history of the *court libraries* (*Hofbibliotheken*) and later *state libraries* (*Landesbibliotheken*) was the transition of having the status of being private property of the ruler to being property of the state as a result of the Revo-

Similar to the English and French models the transition in Germany followed with the change from the "hall library" to the "storage library," the physical division into the reading room, the stacks and the administration succeeded in being accepted. A good example of this is the modern functional architecture of the University Library of Halle (Saxony-Anhalt), (architect: Ludwig von Tiedemann). The upper levels were exclusively available in the storage area; those in the lower levels were only partially in the storage stacks. The Library building, built in 1880, was restored from 1995 – 1999 according to existing regulations for historic monuments.

Today the storage stacks of the University and State Library of Halle (*Universitäts- und Landesbibliothek Halle)* (Saxony-Anhalt) consist of a combination of free-standing iron supports which stretch through four floors and support iron false ceilings and wooden shelves. The open grates of the ceilings allow additional lighting by means of a glass roof.

A German "national" library did not develop out of the Library of the German National Assembly in 1848/49 in St. Paul's Church in Frankfurt – which originally started as a gift of individual publishers – nor out of the Parliamentary Library (*Reichstagsbibliothek*) of the German Empire, founded in 1872. This photo shows the library room in the Parliamentary Building of the German "*Reichstag*" in Berlin (*Bibliothekssaal im Deutschen Reichstag zu Berlin*) about 1895 (architect: Paul Wallot). The room and the collection of the *Reichstagsbibliothek* were destroyed in the Second World War.

tiative of the Association of the German Book Trade (*Börsenvereins der Deutschen Buchhändler*). Thus, at least a central point was created for acquiring of all German-language publications which have been collected in their entirety since 1913 and indexed in the *German National Bibliography* (*Deutsche Nationalbibliographie*).

Already in the second half of the 18th century, reading circles and reading societies, as well as *commercial lending libraries* (*kommerzielle Leih-bibliotheken*), had become the predecessors of public libraries, and had also satisfied the reading interests of the upper middle class society for educational, subject, and entertainment literature. In 1828, a school library was opened in Großenhain in Saxony which later received the charge from the municipality to further education, and is thus recognized today as the first public *city library* (*Stadt-bibliothek*) in Germany.

Motivated by the ideal of general education and through the initiative of liberal societies, churches and the workers' movement in Germany, a wave of library founding in Germany was experienced from the middle of the 19th century. In many cities, librar-

The city of Leipzig, center of book and publishing business in the German Empire, the Kingdom of Saxony, and the Association of the German Book Trade in Leipzig founded the *Deutsche Bücherei* in 1912. Both the interior and exterior architecture of the building on the German Square ("*Deutscher Platz*"), dedicated in 1916, show the influence of the early Italian Renaissance, as well as elements of Art Nouveau (architect's plan: Oskar Pusch).

lution of 1918 – 1919. Of course, even in the times of the monarchs, the court libraries had been opened more and more to the educated public and persons interested in scientific research. Many of these libraries, however, could not keep up with the growing number of publications and thus their development stagnated.

After the French Revolution, the idea of having a "national" library (*Nationalbibliothek*) arose in many of the European countries, but particularly in Germany this idea had no lasting effect – neither in 1848 nor after the founding of the "German Empire" in 1871. The founding of the *Deutsche Bücherei* in Leipzig in 1912 remained a private ini-

The ensemble of buildings belonging to the Library of the Hansa City of Lübeck (*Bibliothek der Hansestadt Lübeck*) in Schleswig-Holstein – a scholarly library with an integrated public library – is comprised of buildings from the Middle Age, as well as from the 19th and 20th centuries. The Neogothic library hall from 1877, which is adjacent to the rooms of the former Franciscan monastery, follows architectural patterns from the Middle Ages.

place. Since many of the previous funding agencies or societies could no longer afford to support them due to the economic development, the entire sphere of public librarianship – to an even greater extent than that of academic libraries – fell under the control and management of the National Socialists after 1933.

The National Socialist government (1933–1945) suppressed the right to free expression, and ended freedom for literature, art and culture, as for all other areas of public life. Nothing illustrates the total claim to power of the Nazi Regime more obviously than the book burning in May 1933, the introduction of censorship, and the flight of a great number of intellectuals into exile. The confessional public libraries belonging to the churches, which had developed since the second half of the 19th century and were supported by the *Borromäusverein (BV)* and the St. Michael's Association in the Catholic Church, as well as by the internal mission of the Protestant Church, were subjected to even stronger repression during the National Socialist period.

ies for the general public (*Volksbüchereien*) were established. However, only under the influence of the American *public libraries* did the concept of a publicly accessible library for all gain acceptance, and led in many places to combining the former city library (*Stadtbibliothek*) and the library for the general public (*Volksbücherei*) to form the so-called "standard library" (*Einheitsbücherei*) or "library for all." There was a "book hall movement" (public library movement) to which such cities as Freiburg, Berlin-Charlottenburg, Essen, and Hamburg (*Hamburger Öffentliche Bücherhallen – HÖB*) belonged as the first cities which hosted public libraries. At the beginning of the 20th century, a countermovement developed because of a discrepancy about the direction such a movement should take. This countermovement aimed at "steering" and teaching the readers, and involved establishing a readers' advisory station at the check-out desk instead of allowing free access to the literature as in the *Einheitsbücherei*.

While in the period of the "Weimar Republic" (1919–1933), a movement to transfer responsibility of the public libraries to the communities (*Kommunalisierung der Volksbüchereien*) took

From Divided to United Germany

The Second World War not only caused enormous damage to the library collections and buildings; its long-term consequences led to the division of Germany and to the far-reaching changes in the library landscape. The collections of the Prussian State Library, which had been evacuated and kept outside of Berlin during the War, were in part returned to Berlin, but remained divided and could only be united almost half a century later. In addition to the *Deutsche Bücherei* in Leipzig, and again on the initiative of the German Book Trade, a West German parallel institution was founded in the *Deutsche Bibliothek* in Frankfurt am Main as the collection point for German literature production and as the national bibliographic center in the West.

Librarianship in higher education experienced a turbulent upturn since the 1960's, which was furthered primarily by the educational expansion beginning at that time. The Federal Republic of Germany experienced a wave of new universities being founded, expansion of existing universities, the establishment of new types of institutions of higher education (*Gesamthochschule*, *Fachhochschule*), and the extension of technical universities to full-fledged universities. The answer to the expansion and differentiation of science and research were also seen in the founding of central subject libraries (*Zentrale Fachbibliotheken*) for the applied sciences (technology, economics / business, medicine and agriculture), as well as the establishment of additional special libraries, the support of librarianship by the German Research Council (*Deutsche Forschungsgemeinschaft*), namely in the sector of cooperative acquisitions in the Special Subject Area Collection Plan (*Sondersammelgebietsplan*), the building of new university libraries with large, freely accessible collections arranged by classification systems, the development of textbook collections and information centers, automation of library work flows and procedures, and networking of all library functions.

Public libraries slowly completed the transition from the ideal of educating the public through the "advisory station" libraries to libraries with free access to the stacks after 1945. In collection development, the previous dominance of *belletristic* literature gave way to more literature for education, vocation and leisure reading; in addition, more non-

fiction and scientific works were acquired, and the collections were rounded out with more types of multimedia. Special departments were established for special user groups, especially for children and youth as an important target group for the public libraries (*Öffentliche Bibliothek* – ÖB). In the large, metropolitan cities, literature provision was expanded to form a system consisting of a central library, branch libraries, and mobile libraries.

Even in public librarianship, new forms of cooperation developed which, however, could not match the extent and intensity that was typical for academic librarianship at this time. But also between these two sectors, cooperation increased, beginning with interlibrary loan. At the latest with the publication of the *Bibliotheksplan '73*, both sectors (academic librarianship and public librarianship) were seen as one unit and efforts toward greater cooperation were slowly intensified.

In the German Democratic Republic (GDR, 1949 – 1990), the second German State, both the State Library in Berlin (*Staatsbibliothek in Berlin*) and the *Deutsche Bücherei* in Leipzig retained their central functions. After elimination of the federated structure in 1952, the regional libraries still in existence at that time were redesigned as so-called *scientific universal libraries* of the regions (*Wissenschaftliche Allgemeinbibliotheken der Bezirke*); only the Saxonian State Library (*Sächsische Landesbibliothek*) in Dresden retained its former name. The public libraries in cities and counties were given the designation "*state general libraries*" (*Staatliche Allgemeinbibliotheken*). By the time the GDR was dissolved, in addition to the libraries of the older universities (Berlin, Greifswald, Halle, Jena, Leipzig, Rostock), over 50 further libraries of institutions of higher education, colleges and engineering schools could be counted, many of which had been newly erected during the GDR period.

The libraries of the research institutes belonging to the Academy of the Sciences and the Central Subject Libraries provided the greatest part of the scientific literature in the GDR. The GDR government pursued its goal of having a library with a full-time professional librarian not only in the cities, but also each community or district was to be provided with a public library and the countryside was to be covered by a complete network of libraries. By the end of the 1980's, over 600 central libraries (*ländliche Zentralbibliotheken*) had been estab-

This wall mural above the circulation desk of the City and State Library Potsdam (*Stadt- und Landesbibliothek Potsdam*) (Brandenburg), a former scientific universal library (*Wissenschaftliche Allgemeinbibliothek*), dates to the 1980's. The main library of the Potsdam Library System has four branch libraries, a slide library and a music library, and contains about 600,000 media units today. Literature about Brandenburg and the Gottfried Benn Collection belong to its special collections.

lished for provision of literature in rural areas. The significance of these libraries in the promotion of reading for children and youth as a meaningful use of leisure time and in the spread of reading and support of reading literacy cannot be underestimated.

The reunification of Germany in 1990 meant an extensive, deep-seated structural change, if not a new beginning for librarianship in the five newly-created Eastern German States and Berlin (taking on their political boundaries from before the War) and did not remain without consequences for librarianship in the Western German States. After being separated for over 40 years, librarianship in West and East Germany grew together again, which is best evidenced in the reunification of libraries. Three libraries today exemplify the situation of one library located on two (in one case even three) places, namely, *Die Deutsche Bibliothek*, which in reunited Germany has taken on the tasks of a national library, the State Library of Berlin –

Prussian Cultural Heritage (*Staatsbibliothek zu Berlin Preußischer Kulturbesitz*) and the Central and State Library of Berlin (*Zentral- und Landesbibliothek Berlin*).

After 1990, great efforts were made to remedy the deficits resulting from the GDR era in both academic and research libraries, and in public libraries. These concerned most importantly changing the physical condition of the library buildings, bringing once separated book collections together again, and obtaining adequate technical equipment.

The Library on the boulevard Unter den Linden, today known as Building 2 of the State Library of Berlin (*Haus 2 der Staatsbibliothek zu Berlin*), has been fully renovated and remodelled over the last few years. It houses the historical collections and special collections, including the largest map collection of the world. This photograph shows a world map from 1633 published in Amsterdam entitled "Atlas, das ist Abbildung der gantzen Welt mit allen darin begriffenen Ländern und Provinzen" (= "Atlas – that is the image of the entire world including all the countries and provinces thereof") by Mercator and Hondius.

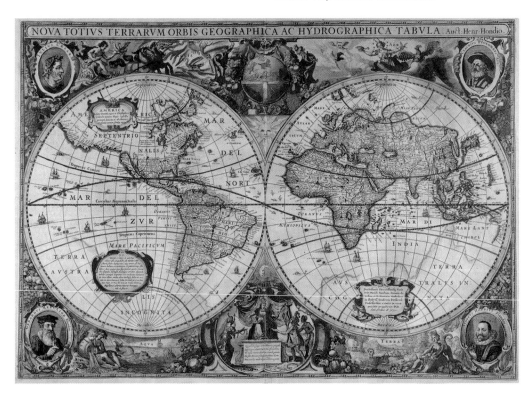

Many library buildings were almost completely renovated during the years from1990 to 2002, and at the same time they were often expanded (the University Library in Leipzig, the main library of the Francke Foundations (*Franckesche Stiftungen*) in Halle, the University and State Library of Halle). Some are still waiting for fundamental renovation (such as the State Library in Berlin, Haus Unter den Linden) or another solution to their space problems (State Library in Schwerin, University Library of the Humboldt University of Berlin). In various cities, new library buildings were built, such as the university libraries in Erfurt, Frankfurt/Oder and Greifswald, the Thuringen University and State Library in Jena, the Saxonian State Library – State and University Library of Dresden and the Library of the University of Applied Sciences in Fürstenwalde. The Duchess Anna Amalia Libary (*Herzogin Anna Amalia Bibliothek*) in Weimar is being renovated and expanded considerably. Numerous public libraries, which in the GDR times had been housed in insufficient buildings with inadequate furnishings and equipment, have received a new home in unused, older buildings in the city centers, for instance, the city libraries in Brandenburg, Eisenach, Fürstenwalde, and Schkeuditz.

The political – ideological orientation of East Germany was reflected in the library collections; many were superfluous and could simply be done without after reunification. On the other hand, fundamental books and journals were not available for many subject areas – in the area of *belletristics* the works of those authors were missing who were officially considered undesirable in the GDR. Academic and research libraries received funding for supplementing their collections soon after reunification from various funding programs while public libraries were essentially left dependent on the modest support from their community funding sources.

In the end, a major goal was to bring the GDR libraries up to the contemporary technological standard as rapidly as possible, to set up self-service copiers (which had not been available before anywhere in the GDR), to introduce data processing and automate library work flow procedures and book processing. Only then could the libraries contribute to the union catalogs and supraregional cooperative ventures for libraries (such as the union catalog for periodicals). Total integration into Ger-

After ten years of restoration work, the University Library in Leipzig (Saxony) could be opened again in 2002. The *Bibliothekca Albertina*, erected in 1891 in the neo-Renaissance style by architect Arwed Rossbach, was two-thirds destroyed by bombing in the final phase of the Second World War and in the following decades was at the mercy of disrepair and deterioration. By placing a roof over the interior courtyards, new reading areas were created. A total of 400,000 volumes are available in open stacks for the users and there are 700 work spaces, some in the reconstructed historic reading room.

man librarianship by means of inclusion in the interlibrary loan network took place almost immediately after Reunification in 1990; only later did participation in the German Research Council (DFG) library special subject areas program take place, as well as in other projects.

In academic and research librarianship, many libraries were completely redesigned and restructured. In addition to the older universities mentioned above, new or rechartered universities, such as in Erfurt, Frankfurt/Oder, Magdeburg and Potsdam, emerged. In the GDR, the type of institution known in West Germany as the "*Fachhochschule*" was introduced in the former GDR after 1991. The Academy of the Sciences in Berlin and Leipzig with its libraries and archives were completely newly established. East German Central Libraries were virtually deprived of their function as the parallel institutions in West Germany were disproportionately better stocked. The same was true for many administrative libraries. After the scientific general libraries were dissolved, the state libraries were separated from the respective local city libraries and took over regional functions for the states (*Länder*) which were redefined in the 1990's; in Federal *Länder* without a state library the regional tasks fell to the university libraries – a double function which is evident also in the their names (such as in Halle/Saxony-Anhalt, Jena/Thuringia). The Saxonian State Library in Dresden was joined with the Library of the Dresden Technical University in1996 and physically combined with it in 2002 in a new building.

More than the academic and research libraries (*Wissenschaftliche Bibliotheken – WB*), the city libraries, which had come under city administration after 1990, fell into a crisis situation as a result of the difficult economic situation of the public budgets. In particular, the smaller libraries in the country and the almost 3,000 libraries of the unions and companies – both those headed by full-time library staff or even by volunteers – had to be closed. However, a certain balance was achieved through the implementation of many new mobile libraries in rural areas. A strict reduction of staff started in libraries, as had already taken place in government offices and companies. The demand for "other" literature and new media could – at first – only be met with great difficulty. The state service centers for public libraries (*Staatliche Büchereifachstellen*) – completely unheard of in the GDR – had to be newly established and in the years following, they took on the task of systematically redeveloping the public libraries, thus providing many new impulses for adapting to the same professional standards in all the states of former West and East Germany.

The German Library Institute (*Deutsches Bibliotheksinstitut – DBI*) in Berlin played an instrumental role in the integration of West German and East German librarianship. It had been founded in 1978 on the basis of a law creating this Institute and after the Reunification of Germany, it was expanded to include the corresponding parallel Institute existing in the former GDR. Its objective was to provide supraregional (national) services for practical application in all the various types of libraries, as well as to further application-oriented research and development in the area of librarianship. Its tasks included cooperative projects in the area of data processing, marketing services, continuing educational activities, comprehensive professional commissions for major activities, carrying out, monitoring and publishing reports on library projects in the national and European level, the production and publication of the German Library Statistics (*Deutsche Bibliotheksstatistik – DBS*), the publication of an abstract and review documentation for the field of librarianship (*Dokumentation für Bibliotheken – DOBI*), as well as the promotion of international contacts.

This Institute, which had been jointly financed by the Federal Government and the states was, as a result of a recommendation by the Scientific Council (*Wissenschaftsrat*) dissolved on January 1, 2000, by law. After three years of organizing its dissolution, its activities were ended on December 31, 2002. With this, German librarianship lost its only centrally positioned, governmental institution for library infrastructure. Some of the tasks taken on by the DBI, such as the technical management of the database of the Union Catalog of Periodicals (*Zeitschriftendatenbank*) and the publication of the professional journal *Bibliotheksdienst*, have been continued by other institutions, but other tasks have had to be completely terminated. All the efforts to establish a new innovative service center for German librarianship have remained unsuccessful thusfar. But the German Library Association (DBV) is still advocating a network of competencies for selected services to be jointly financed by the *Länder* (*Kompetenznetzwerk*).

2 EDUCATION AND CULTURE

Germany's Political, Administrative and Organizational Development

Fundamental knowledge of the political, administrative and organizational development of Germany and its school and higher education system is an important prerequisite for understanding the structure and organization of German librarianship.

The Federal Republic of Germany was founded in May 1949, four years after the end of the Second World War, as a federated country on the basis of a democratic, parliamentarian foundation. After Reunification of the two German countries on October 3, 1990, it now consists of 16 *Länder*: the large-area *Länder* Baden-Württemberg, Bavaria, Brandenburg, Hesse, Mecklenburg-Western Pommerania, Lower Saxony, North Rhine-Westphalia, the Rhineland-Palatinate, the Saarland, Saxony, Saxony-Anhalt, Schleswig-Holstein and Thuringia, as well as the city-states of Berlin, Bremen and Hamburg. The capital city of Germany is Berlin.

Some statistics (as of December 31, 2002)	
Total Population (Residents):	82,444,000 inhabitants
Percentage of Foreigners:	9.4 %
Area:	357,020 square kilometres (km)
Population Density:	235 inhabitants per square km
Number of Cities and Communities:	14,895
Gross National Product per Inhabitant:	17,200 Euros
Percentage of Unemployed:	10.9%

The fundamental basis for the constitutional regulations in Germany is the Basic Law (*Grundgesetz – GG*). The principle of the Federal state provides the possibility to place state tasks at the level of the *Länder* and the communities, which allows greater consideration of regional features and needs.

The constitutional organs of the Federal Government and the *Länder* correspond to the division of powers:
· the Federal and state Parliaments (*Bundestag, Landtage*)
· the President of the Federal Republic, the Federal Government, the governments of the *Länder*
· the Federal Courts and the state courts (*Landesgerichte*).

The parliamentarian system of the Federal Republic of Germany allows two representations: the directly elected popular representation with ca. 600 delegates (*Bundestag*) and the representation of the individual *Länder* (*Bundesrat*), which are sent by the governments of the 16 *Länder*. The *Bundesrat* is actively involved especially in creating laws which primarily affect the basic interests of the *Länder*. The guidelines of German politics and the appointment of the Federal ministers determine the Federal Chancellor (*Bundeskanzler*). The head of state, the *Bundespräsident*, is not directly elected by the populace, but rather through the Federal Assembly (*Bundesversammlung)*; members of this unit include all delegates of the Federal Parliament, all representatives of the *Bundesrat* and in a smaller

The 16 *Länder* of the Federal Republic of Germany with their capital cities and shields

number, persons involved in public life as determined by the political parties.

According to the Basic Law (*Grundgesetz*), state and administration are constituted from the lower level to the top level, that is from the communities (*Gemeinde*) to the *Länder* up to the Federal Government (*Bund*). The process of making a law (*Gesetzgebung*) for regional activities rests with the individual *Länder*, though national tasks remain the responsibility of the Federal Government. The Basic Law is supplemented by the Unification Contract (*Einigungsvertrag*) from August 32, 1990, between the German Democratic Republik (GDR) and the Federal Republic of Germany and is also relevant to librarianship in Germany. Administrative activities (*Verwaltungstätigkeit*) are primarily carried out by the communities and the *Länder*. Legal jurisdiction is primarily the task of the *Länder* or rather, the state courts (*Landesgerichte*). In contrast to this are the institutions of the Federal Supreme Court. The highest of these courts is the Federal Constitutional Court (*Bundesverfassungsgericht*) in Karlsruhe. The communities, *Länder* and Federal Government each have their own jurisdiction and the *Länder* also have their own constitutions. They rely on income from the part of the revenues (*Steueraufkommen*) allotted to them.

The responsibility for all cultural affairs, for science and the arts, as well as for schools and education, lies fundamentally with the *Länder*. The cities and communities also have part in this "cultural jurisdiction" in context of the prescriptions for municipal code and regulations of the respective states which exercise their own jurisdiction (= cultural autonomy of the municipalities – *kommunale Kulturautonomie*). A "library law" does not exist in Germany, nor does a central Federal cultural ministry, although since 1998 the Federal Government has attempted to bundle its various cultural tasks under the responsibility of a state minister as "the Federal commissioner of all affairs of culture and media" (*Beauftragter der Bundesregierung für Angelegenheiten der Kultur und der Medien*). In the coming years, these efforts of the Federal Government may be strengthened so as to exercise greater central influence on the basic conditions and policies for cultural and education more intensively than before.

Since certain projects in the area of education, science and research have national significance, the

Administrative Structure of a Federal State
(*Bundesland*)

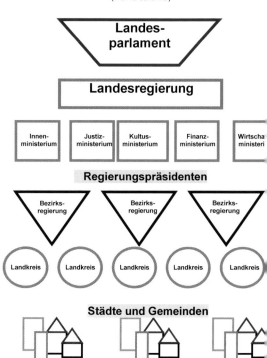

English terms for diagram p. 11

Federal Government promotes and finances such so-called common community goals (*Gemeinschaftsaufgaben*) within certain limits. Such goals are anchored in the Basic Law and affect primarily the extension and construction of new institutions of higher education, as well as the "Framework Agreement for Furthering Research" (*Rahmenvereinbarung Forschungsförderung*) concerning the Scientific Association Gottfried Wilhelm Leibniz – WGL (*Wissenschaftsgemeinschaft Gottfried Wilhelm Leibniz – WGL*). Some of the institutions and agreements established by the Federal State Government and the *Länder* are also significant for librarianship: The Federal Ministry for Education and Research (BMBF), the German Research Council (*Deutsche Forschungsgemeinschaft*) (DFG), as well as several database and pilot projects, including the Information and Documentation (*IuD-Programm*) Program for the Advancement of Information and Documentation, the development of

Digital Libraries (*Digitale Bibliotheken*), as well as the continued development of the subject-oriented information centers (*Fachinformationszentren*). From 1978 until 2002, many of these areas of responsibility belonged to the German Library Institute (*Deutsches Bibliotheksinstitut* – DBI) which was included in the so-called "Blue List" (*Blaue Liste*) of research institutions according to the "Framework Agreement for Furthering Research" to give "extensive research support".

The passing of laws in the individual Federal *Länder* is the task of the parliaments, which in the large area states are called *Landtage*, in the City-States (Hamburg, Bremen, Berlin) the House of Delegates (*Abgeordnetenhaus* or *Bürgerschaft*). The *Länder* are governed politically and administratively by the individual state governments (*Landesregierungen*), which are headed by a minister president (*Ministerpräsident*) or governing mayor (*Regierender Bürgermeister*). Within an 8 to 10 member cabinet (called the Senate – *Senat*), there are usually the cultural ministries (*Kultusministerien*) or ministries of science (*Wissenschaftsministerien*) who are respectively responsible for public librarianship or for academic and research librarianship of that *Land*. In the larger Federal *Länder*, state intermediary administrators are under the supervision of the governing president of the *Land* and have administrative authority for certain parts of that *Land* (the so-called governmental precincts – *Regierungsbezirke*). One of the significant tasks of these authorities is the state supervision of the communities (*Kommunalaufsicht*). In most of the *Länder*, State Service Centers for Public Libraries (*Staatlichen Büchereistellen*), also called professional centers (*Fachstellen)*, counselling centers (*Beratungsstellen*), library centers (*Büchereizentralen*), have been established. Their influence remains primarily within the political administrative units (counties, precincts, etc.).

In the large-area states with sparse population, the counties (*Landkreise*) and the cities without counties (*kreisfreie Städte*) or cities whose borders also represent counties (*Stadtkreise*) take on – in addition to their original task of maintaining a self-sufficient administration – the additional function of a subordinate state administrative agency.

Fundamentally, the cities and communities are responsible for all public duties in their territory inasmuch as the Land or Federal law does not state or otherwise prescribe other regulations. Certain obligatory tasks (*Pflichtaufgaben)* fall to the community administration – for instance, the execution of social welfare assistance, the establishment of primary and secondary schools and the so-called "voluntary" (*freiwillige*) or freely designable tasks with no legal obligations: Among these are the entire area of culture affecting the maintenance of theaters, orchestras, museums and libraries. Through the county elections, political representatives (*politische Gemeindevertreter*) are elected, such as the community council (*Gemeinderat*), the city council (*Stadtrat*), or the mayor (*Bürgermeister*), who delegate committees for the individual tasks; usually, a cultural committee (*Kulturausschuss*) is politically responsible for community libraries. A community administration is divided – depending on the size of the community and its organizational structure – into departments (*Dezernate*), subject areas (*Fachbereiche*) and Offices (*Ämter*). The community public library can thereby be an independent city unit or be assigned to the school or cultural department as a dependent institution. Museums, archives, community colleges, and music schools (academies) can also be treated in a similar manner.

Various income taxes cover the financial needs of the Federal Republic, the *Länder* and the communities. The communities and the *Länder* receive free as well as certain specifically allocated percentages of the entire tax revenues. The communities can also determine their own community taxes, such as corporate taxes, or property tax, assessments and fees, while the counties can only be financed through the annually apportioned taxes of the communities belonging to the county. The expenses for the community- and state-supported libraries are covered by the comprehensive tax revenues. The amount of the expenditures and income sources are decided annually by the parliaments and recorded in the budgets.

Educational Institutions

General Education Schools

German education is particularly moulded through the federative structure of Germany. The predominant majority of the schools and higher education institutions are public institutions. Within the educational and cultural politics of the states (*Länder*), schools and educational institutions are legally anchored and with their traditionally strong distinctive pedagogical and instructional functions thus naturally enjoy a higher standing than libraries. In context of their independence in educational and cultural matters, the *Länder* regulate all legislation for education and instruction. Financially, most schools are supported by the communities and combined communities; a small number of schools are supported privately or by church entities. While the financial supporter of the school must pay the operating costs (building, furnishings and overhead), the *Länder* bear the costs of the instructional staff.

Fundamental Elements of the Tree-Tiered School System in Germany

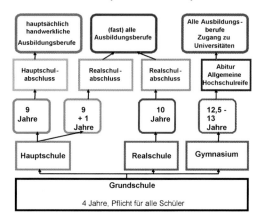

English terms for diagram p. 11

School Form (see footnotes)	Schools Total / Percentage	Teachers Number / Percentage	Pupils Number / Percentage	Foreign Pupils
Grundschulen	17,275 = 36.7%	191,102 = 28.5%	3.4 Mio. = 33.7%	11.8%
Hauptschulen	5,657 = 13.6%	73,225 = 10.9%	1.1 Mio. = 11.1%	17.3%
Realschulen	3,469 = 8.3%	74,753 = 11.1%	1.3 Mio. = 12.7%	6.4%
Gymnasien	3,166 = 7.6%	152,775 = 22.7%	2.3 Mio. = 22.7%	3.9%
Gesamtschulen	788 = 1.9%	42,495 = 6.3%	0.5 Mio. = 5.5%	12.0%
Sonderschulen	3,123 = 7.5%	67,232 = 10.0%	0. Mio. = 4.2%	14.9%
Total	41,633	671,500	9.96 Million	Average 11 %

Source: Destabis, Date: 1 Mar 2001, *Spiegel Spezial* 3/2002.

[1] The *Volksschule* or *Grundschule* are the primary schools (elementary levels) and range from the introductory year of "*Vorschule*" (equivalent to the American "kindergarten") prior to the first grade through grade 4 (in Berlin through grade 6).

[2] *Hauptschule* can be translated as "middle school," but it is often also the final school for pupils who begin a practical training course (usually vocational training). This level of school ends with the 10th grade.

[3] *Realschule* can be translated as "junior high school," as many students also attend until the 10th grade and then participate in a vocational training course (usually the dual system of on-the-job training combined with the theoretical technical school training).

[4] *Gymnasium* is the secondary school form which includes grades 5–13 (in Berlin grades 7–13) and is the only school form to offer a pre-university track. It is said to be equivalent to the British "grammar school."

[5] *Gesamtschule* is translated as "Comprehensive Secondary School." It is usually a full day school, as opposed to the other schools at the secondary level.

[6] *Sonderschulen* are schools for special education of all types. There are, however, specific schools for pupils with various types of physical handicaps, mental and learning handicaps, blindness, etc. They include all ages and are usually instructed according to ability and progressive performance as opposed to age and grade level.

From *Land* to *Land* there are differences in the organization and development of the school systems – each according to the political orientation of the current government. In order to establish a minimum national standard across the country, the Standing Committee of the Cultural Ministers of the *Länder* (*Ständige Konferenz der Kultusminister der Länder* – KMK) functions as a mediating authority: For instance, the KMK decrees recommendations on the length of the school year, the components of the curriculum, the evaluation of school performance or the reciprocal recognition of examinations and grades. A similar role is played by the Conference of Vice-Chancellors (*Hochschulrektorenkonferenz* – HRK) for institutions of higher education.

There are a total of 41,600 schools in Germany with about 671,500 teachers and almost 10 million pupils with an average of 11 % foreign pupils.

Attending school is free in all *Länder*. This also applies in general for attending a higher educational institution, as long as certain regular time periods of study are not exceeded. *Mandatory school attendance* requires all children from the age of 6 to the age of 18 to attend school. After attending the elementary school (usually for four years), the pupil transfers to schools that take their pupils to higher levels than the minimum requirements of compulsory school attendance. In addition, there are the higher levels *Hauptschule* (Middle School) *Realschule* (Junior High School) and *Gymnasium* (secondary, university preparation school). Only in a few of the German *Länder* do "comprehensive schools" (*Gesamtschulen*) exist, in which the various types of secondary schools are integrated. Pupils who begin a vocational training program are required to attend a vocational school (*Berufsschule*). Central school libraries with adequate equipment and collections exist only in a small number of the primary schools, but they do exist in most of the *Gymnasien* and *Gesamtschulen*.

Vocational Training

The "Vocational Training Act" (*Berufsbildungsgesetz*) regulates the basis and the principles for vocational training in Germany. The major component and main characteristic of the first vocational training in almost all branches of the trades being learned is the so-called "dual system" (*Duales System*); it is based upon the cooperation between two totally different financiers of education – on the one hand the *private businesses,* on the other hand, the *publicly funded vocational training schools.* While the communities bear the costs of the vocational training schools and the *Länder* have responsibility for designing the instruction, the Federal Government is also involved in vocational training, specifically in the development of general requirements for the individual professions (i.e., a professional training framework). The responsibility for controlling the transfer of learning according to the state-prescribed directives within the internal training process in the businesses lies with the chambers of commerce (*Industrie- und Handelskammer)* and the trade corporations (*Handwerkskammer*). Employers' associations and trade unions agree in corresponding committees on the formulation of the content of the individual training programs for the distinct professions.

Most youth begin their training after completion of the middle school (*Hauptschule*), the junior high school level (*Realschule*) or the grammar school level (*Gymnasium*) whereby the training course always consists of a required number of vocational school instruction in the required subjects for that trade in addition to on-the-job training. The trainee signs a contract which requires the employer to provide the youth with the necessary time to attend the vocational school instruction. The training period usually lasts three years. At the end of the training time, the trainees must pass an examination which is administered by an authorized, independent institution, most usually a chamber of commerce or trade corporation. The certificate of successful completion is generally recognized within the respective professional field.

In librarianship at this time, there is only one profession for which a vocational training program according to the dual system is allowed, and which as of 1999 has superceded the earlier profession of "library assistant" (*Assistent an Bibliotheken*): In a three-year training program, trainees who have completed any of the secondary school levels (*Hauptschule*, *Realschule* and *Gymnasium*) can be trained for the profession of "professional skilled employee for media and information service" (*Fachangestellter für Medien- und Informationsdienste*) in one of five different areas of specialty.

Photo and Film Services for Teachers and Media Centers

With the rising significance of audiovisual and digital media in the field of education, the sphere of activities of the so-called "photo and film service units" (*Bildstellen*) and "media centers" (*Medienzentren*) in the educational field which had evolved in Germany during the 1930's also grew.

Today there are approximately 600 media centers financed by cities and counties, as well as 15 state media centers (*Landesmedienzentren*) which primarily support the media work of the schools and school libraries and make important contributions to the improvement of media competencies of both pupils and teachers. These institutions are responsible for the purchase and provision of audiovisual media, their cataloging and classification for instructional purposes, consultation regarding the use and purchase of audiovisual media (videos, films, DVDs, educational software, CD-ROMs) and AV-devices (video recorder, digital cameras, film projectors, PCs), as well as for the transfer of knowledge on media didactics and the influence and effects of media. As a partner of the schools, and increasingly also of school libraries and public

The Ruhr University in Bochum (*Ruhr-Universität Bochum*) (North Rhine-Westphalia), founded in 1962 and opened in 1965, is the first newly-founded university in the Federal Republic of Germany (after World War II) and at the same time a model example of university architecture since the 1960's. The University Library lies exactly in the middle between the buildings of the faculties. With 1.2 million volumes, it offers its entire book collection in open access stacks with 400 work spaces for users.

libraries, they are important places for first-level information for learning critical as well as creative integration and use of the modern media forms.

Professional Continuing Education and Further Education

Continuing professional education and further education in Germany has two main objectives: first, previously attained professional qualifications can be brought up to date in terms of the newest technological and work-oriented, organizational developments, and secondly, they serve to expand and deepen professional knowledge. Commercial enterprises are the most important financers of professional continuing education. Only in a few areas of further education is the state directly involved – to these belong those institutions under responsibility of the *Länder*, such as the technical colleges (*Fachschulen*) with their diverse courses of study and training courses. In addition to the companies and technical colleges, there is an entire market of private continuing education vendors, for example the technical academies (*Technische Akademien*), the training centers of businesses (*Bildungswerke der Wirtschaft*) or the professional continuing educa-

The County Library of Aurich (*Landschaftsbibliothek Aurich*) (Lower Saxony), founded in 1600, maintains a special collection area literature about the county, and thus functions as the regional library (*Regionalbibliothek*) for East Friesland. The annex, built in 1995, has received several prizes and added an area of open stacks to the building erected in 1964 which otherwise had only closed stacks.

tion centers of the trade unions (*Berufsfortbildungswerke der Gewerkschaften*). Only in librarianship can more than 25 state- or privately-owned organizations be found nationwide with a comparatively comprehensive offering of continuing education events.

Adult Education and Community Colleges

In addition to the professional further education possibilities, adult education (*Erwachsenenbildung*) plays a significant role as one of the components of general education. Adult education – in contrast to school education – is almost totally free of state control or supervision. The most important financers of adult education are the community colleges (*Volkshochschulen* – VHS), which have existed in Germany for about 80 years. Today there are about 1,000 community colleges which are supported by the communities, counties, churches, trade unions, and private societies. The VHS has no limits in the topics they offer nor in the type of participants. However, there is a charge for taking part in the courses. In addition, numerous private and state-supported institutions offer distance learning courses; in the last three to four years, the use of Internet-based courses has increased both in volume and in significance.

Cooperation between municipal public libraries and the institutions offering adult education is relatively underdeveloped. In some places, however, one finds promising attempts, occasionally where the director of the community college and the public library are the same person or where there is even joint accommodation in one building. The spatial consolidation enables the creation of "self-learning centers" (*Selbstlernzentren*), which have been established as pilot projects in several cities.

Universities and other Higher Education Institutions

In Germany, about 1.9 million students attend approximately 250 German universities and institutions of higher education. To these institutions for research, teaching and study belong – in addition to 79 universities – 20 consolidated universities (*Gesamthochschulen*), technical universities, con-

servatories for fine arts (*Kunsthochschulen*) and theological seminaries (*Theologische Hochschulen*), the two universities of the German Federal Armed Forces, as well as 156 universities of applied sciences *(Fachhochschulen)*. They are for the most part state institutions financed by the *Länder*. In addition to those, increasing numbers of private foundations or business enterprises are sponsoring and establishing institutions of higher education with special operational profiles, instructional offerings and degree programs. University instructors and other staff of state institutions are employed as civil servants and employees of public service. Thanks to the autonomy of the universities (*Hochschulautonomie*), institutions of higher education have the right to independently decree important regulations, for instance, examination regulations. For all other purposes, the Federal Parliament "Act for General Higher Education" (*Hochschulrahmen-*

The Business and Economics Science Branch Library (*Wirtschaftswissenschaftliche Zweigbibliothek*) of the *University Library of Eichstätt* in Ingolstadt (Bavaria), seat of one of the 53 European Documentation Centers (EDZ) in Germany, was opened in 1989 in a reconstructed former seminary of the Styler missionaries. A reading room and a five-storey shelving unit (book tower) for the open access stacks have been built in the former church nave with choir and gallery,.

gesetz – HRG) provides guidance. Furthermore, research assistance, higher education entrance, and educational assistance for students (Bafög) is regulated by Federal law; as the basis of the "Act for Building Assistance for Institutions of Higher Education" (Hochschulbauförderungsgesetzes – HBFG), the Federal government contributes 50% of the costs for the construction of buildings of an institution of higher education and its first basic equipment with computer technology and scientific literature.

While the universities and institutions of higher education in the United States are given ca. 1.1% of the gross domestic product (Bruttoinlandsprodukt) as public expenditure in Germany and a further 1.2% from donations, approximately 1% is obtained from pubic funds and 0.1% comes from donations; in Sweden and Finland the costs are distributed quite differently: there is 0% from private sponsors and 0.1% from public funds , but for the most part in these countries, the entire budget takes in 1.7% of the gross domestic product.

Libraries of institutions of higher education are integrated relatively tightly into the university structures through appropriate laws, acts, and statutes of the Länder and thus their existence is assured. On the other hand, current developments in several of the Federal states have placed these basic principles somewhat into question. Libraries of institutions of higher education serve primarily the instructors of the institution and the students; today, though they are also open to the general public.

In Germany, the following types of institutions of higher education have developed:

· Universities, Technical Universities and Comprehensive Universities (Gesamthochschulen): The entrance requirements for studying at a university or equivalent institution of higher education is the general or subject oriented "matriculation requirement" (Hochschulreife), which is usually attained after 13 years of school. The actual length of study consists of 6 years, although the usual length of study for most of the subject areas is four-and-a-half years. The largest universities, based on student population, are in Berlin (three universities with a total of 110,000 students), Cologne (64,000 students), Munich and Münster (both with 44,000 students), Hamburg (40,000 students) and Bonn (38,000 students).

· Specialized Institutions of Higher Education (Fachhochschulen): The courses of study at the 156 Fachhochschulen in Germany differ from the courses of study at the universities by nature of the greater application and practical orientation. The usual length of study lies between three and four years, the actual length of study is hardly above that. An average of 25–28% of all students decide to study at a Fachhochschule.
· Academies or Colleges of Art (Kunsthochschulen): Different institutions of higher education are available for the formative arts, design, music, film and television. Acceptance to these courses of study is based on a qualification test for that subject area.

In some Länder other types of institutions of higher education exist, such as teachers' colleges (teacher training) and professional academies (for instance, special study at a technical college to accompany employment in a profession).

To summarize, German education shows two unique features when compared internationally. First, the independence in educational and cultural matters of the Länder (Kulturhoheit), based on the federalism in Germany, allows an extensive independent development and organization of general education. Secondly, the legislation entrusts businesses with a part of the vocational training by turning over to them the practical part of the professional training for the firstlearned profession. Education in Germany is characterized especially by a high degree of internal institutional openness towards individual educational needs. Its goal is to allow professional mobility, transparency and equal opportunity. Thus, in the meantime, it is no longer unusual that former graduates of the middle school have attained additional qualifications and are able to complete university study later. In the tertiary level of education (tertiärer Bildungssektor) two types of institutions of higher education are in competition, whereby the shorter and more practical courses of study at the Fachhochschulen have won greater appeal for the practical professions in comparison to university courses of study.

The Book Trade

The book trade represents one of the most important partners of libraries. In Germany, the book trade rests on a tradition which reaches back into

Börsenverein des Deutschen Buchhandels e.V.

the Middle Ages. This tradition not only possesses outstanding cultural importance, but also evidences a significant economic factor.

Of the 3,741 statistically recorded book publishers, the 5,223 book sellers and the over 80 intermediate book trade dealers, a large portion (6,751 companies) belong to the Association of the German Book Trade (*Börsenverein des Deutschen Buchhandels e.V.*). This central association of book producers and sellers, founded in Leipzig in 1825, has its headquarters today in Frankfurt am Main. Since 1949, the International Frankfurt Book Fair (*Internationale Frankfurter Buchmesse*) takes place there annually, the largest book fair of the world. Each year the renowned Peace Prize of the German Book Trade (*Friedenspreis des Deutschen Buchhandels*) is awarded there. The Association publishes a professional journal, the *Börsenblatt des Deutschen Buchhandels*, which not only advertises new books, but also contains editorial contributions on the world of the book. The publishing house of the Association of the German Book Trade also publishes the *German Books in Print* (*Verzeichnis Lieferbarer Bücher – VLB*), which informs book dealers and libraries on all available titles including their prices.

As in many other countries, in Germany books have fixed retail prices, which is not the case for any other product because of market economy reasons. The system of collective guarantee for the sale of fixed-price publications, which in the past had been organized on a private or basically voluntary basis, was dissolved in October 2002 by a law which required retailers to set fixed prices and inform the buyers about this price. Deviations from the fixed prices are only allowed in certain cases. One of those is the library discount which allows a 5% discount for all publicly accessible academic and research libraries and 10% for public libraries including school libraries.

The price-fixing for books guarantees a diversity of titles which exceeds that of any other country of the world with the exception of Great Britain. Despite the advances made by new media, book production in the past rose continuously and in 2001, 90,000 new titles appeared, of which 68,400 were first editions. Among the new titles, *belletristic*

titles take first place (14%), but also children's and youth literature is well-represented (7%), followed by the other subject areas, such as business, medicine, law, etc. The greatest number of new books are published in Munich, but Berlin, Frankfurt/Main, Stuttgart, Cologne, and Hamburg are important publishing locations. These cities are also those which have the highest number of book stores.

The number of translations may be considered an indicator in determining the cultural openness of a country. Approximately every seventh book published in Germany in 2001 was translated into German from another language. Among the original languages, English dominates (74%), with French following at a large distance (8.8%) and after that Italian (3 %). Especially high is the number of translations in *belletristic*, but there is also a considerable number of translations of children's and youth books and comics. Based on the number of requests for licensing translation of German titles in other countries, the opening of the East indicates an orientation towards world economics: Chinese, Spanish, and Korean translations of German books rank even before the number of English translations. Numerous books, however, are also translated into Italian, Czech, French, Polish, Dutch and Russian.

3 THE VARIETY OF LIBRARIES

The Multifaceted Picture of Libraries in Germany

The Variety of Funding Institutions

Among the characteristics which have influenced German librarianship is the variety of different library types. Not infrequently, these library types have their origins in a specific historical era, thus they are closely bound with the cultural and intellectual development of Germany and its territories. Most often they can be arranged according to a specific type of funding institution. Therefore, it seems reasonable to cast a glance on the different types of funding institutions for libraries and name the most important of these: the *public funding institutions* (öffentliche), the *religious funding institutions* (kirchliche) and the *private funding institutions* (private).

Public Funding Institutions

The Federal Government

Die Deutsche Bibliothek is primary among the libraries financed by the Federal government. In reunified Germany, it takes on the function of a national library. However, also of considerable significance are the Library of the German Parliament (*Bibliothek des Deutschen Bundestages*) with 1.3 million volumes and one of the largest parliamentary libraries in the entire world, the libraries of the Federal Ministries, the administrative libraries, the libraries of the Federal courts and of the Federal research institutions, as well as the two universities of the German Armed Forces in Hamburg and Neubiberg (near Munich).

Since the responsibility for science, education, culture and art is reserved almost exclusively for the *Länder*, the Federal Government only acts in a few isolated cases as the library funding agency.

However, the Federal Government participates in financing individual libraries and institutions with supraregional (national) significance. The approximately 80 research institutions not connected to universities, which have joined together in the *Scientific Association Gottfried Wilhelm Leibniz* (*Wissenschaftsgemeinschaft Gottfried Wilhelm Leibniz*) are jointly funded by the Federal Government and the *Länder* and correspondingly have their own special libraries. Other institutions which belong to the scientific and research infrastructure are also members of the Leibniz Society including the Central Subject Libraries for Medicine, Technology and Business-Economics. A mixture of financing – from the Federal Government, private foundations and the individual *Länder* – is evidenced in the large research institutions such as the *Max Planck Society*, the *Fraunhofer Society* or the *Hermann von Helmholtz Association of German Research Centers*, which also maintain important special libraries.

The *Länder*

Because of the fundamental principles of the above-mentioned cultural and educational autonomy of the states for decision-making in matters of science, education and social aspects (*Kulturhoheit*), the *Länder* are the most important funding bodies in Germany of the academic and research libraries. The Federal States already have the responsibility for almost all institutions of higher education and thus also for the university libraries – with the exception of the state parliamentary libraries (*Landtagsbibliotheken*), the state libraries (*Landesbibliotheken*) and the regional libraries (*Regionalbibliotheken*).

The Municipalities

The most important funding agencies for the public libraries are the cities and the communities which can make use of the legally embodied right to self-government within the community to maintain a city library or a community library, which in many instances they do. In some Federal states, the counties also support a central county library or multi-county library which is also sometimes organized as a mobile library, or they commit to financially subsidizing the city and community libraries in close proximity.

Foundations under Public Law

Several public foundations are financial supporters of important libraries. Among these are above all the Foundation of the Prussian Cultural Heritage (*Stiftung Preußischer Kulturbesitz*) with the State Library in Berlin (*Staatsbibliothek zu Berlin*) and the Foundation of the Weimar Classic (*Stiftung Weimarer Klassik)* with the Duchess Anna Amalia Library (*Herzogin Anna Amalia Bibliothek*) in Weimar. Additional foundations under public law, which maintain their own libraries and therefore are dependent on the financial subsidies of the regional corporate bodies, are the Francke Foundations (*Franckeschen Stiftungen*) in Halle on the Saale River with its so-called main library, the Foundation of the Germanic National Museum (*Stiftung Germanisches Nationalmuseum*) in Nuremberg with its significant special library, and the Foundation of the Central and State Library Berlin (*Stiftung Zentral- und Landesbibliothek Berlin)*, under whose auspices the Berlin City Library (*Stadtbibliothek*) and the American Memorial Library (*Amerika-Gedenk-Bibliothek – AGB)* are united.

Religious Funding Institutions

Both the Catholic and the Protestant Church maintain a large number of libraries. The cathedral, diocesan, and state church libraries belong to the classification of scholarly *special libraries*, along with the libraries of the seminaries and other religious institutions and associations. In addition, the libraries of non-secular institutions of higher education make up an integral component of academic and research librarianship, such as that of the Catholic University Eichstätt (*Katholische Universität Eichstätt*). Small *public libraries*, mostly headed by volunteers, are supported by the local churches by the parishes and church congregations. In many

The Central Library of the Catholic University Eichstätt (*Zentralbibliothek der Katholischen Universität Eichstätt*) in Bavaria was given a new building (architect: Günter Behnisch) in the Auen countryside of the Altmühl in 1987. The building is completely transparent, and forms and figures play into one another – an award-winning building because of its high design value and the experiential nature of its architecture. Among the furniture for library patrons are carrels which enable concentrated work, but at the same time allow a view towards the river.

The Court Library of the Prince of Thurn and Taxis (*Fürst Thurn und Taxis Hofbibliothek*) in Regensburg (Bavaria), belongs to the category "private libraries" and is a scholarly universal library with 212,000 volumes, 350 manuscripts, and 1,700 incunabula and early imprints which had been made available to the public as early as 1782. The Baroque domed hall, built in 1732 and named after its painter Cosmas Damian Asam, houses the older collections of the Library.

rural regions, the church libraries fulfill the tasks of general literature provision, due to the lack of community-maintained institutions.

Private Funding Institutions

Private funding institutions of libraries include companies and societies, as well as private persons. Many large businesses maintain their own libraries and information centers for purposes of research and development and which focus specifically on the literature needs of the company workers. These Libraries are generally not open to the public. Also belonging to the category of scientific special libraries are the libraries which have been developed by associations with economic, professional, scientific or idealistic objectives to support their work. Private persons as the owners of larger libraries which are open to the public have become much rarer in Germany than in the past. Only in exceptional instances have private collections remained in the hands of the nobility (Regensburg, Sigmaringen).

Variety of Types of Libraries

The individual types of libraries can be differentiated not only according to their funding institutions – public or private financiers – but also according to their historical development, their size and the areas of emphasis of their collections, and according to the particular user groups. Fundamental differentiation criteria are the respective objectives and functions. In reality, there are numerous areas of overlapping functions, especially in libraries with dual functions as indicated even in their names (i.e., City and State Library: "*Stadt- und Landesbibliothek*"). Therefore, in the following sections, the emphasis will be on the central function of the library as the characteristic factor.

Libraries with National Significance

In contrast to many other countries no national library was formed for a long period of time in Germany because of the territorial fragmentation and internal political contradictions. The *Deutsche Bücherei*, founded by the Association of the German Book Trade with support of the city of Leipzig and the Kingdom of Saxony in 1912, could not ful-

fill its tasks of being a national library and center for national bibliography for the Western parts ("*Zonen*") of Germany after the division of Germany in 1945. Thus, on the initiative of publishers and librarians, *Die Deutsche Bibliothek* was created in 1946 in Frankfurt on the Main. At the time of reunification of Germany in1990, both these institutions were joined together. The newly created institution carries the name *Die Deutsche Bibliothek* (DDB). Though its tasks are distributed in three different places, Leipzig, Frankfurt am Main, and Berlin, where the German Music Archives (*Deutsches Musikarchiv*), established in 1970, are located, these three institutions combine to fulfill many of the responsibilities of a national library.

Die Deutsche Bibliothek

With approximately 18 million media units, of which nine million are in Leipzig, eight million in Frankfurt am Main and one million sets of sheet music and recordings in Berlin, *Die Deutsche Bibliothek* is by far the largest library in Germany. Its legal task since 1913 is the collection, archiving, and bibliographical indexing of

· All items published, printed or electronically, in Germany, totally independent of their medium, including publications on the Internet
· German-language publications published in another country
· German-language items translated into another language and published abroad
· Publications in other languages about Germany (Germanica) published abroad
· All printed items published or written by German emigrants from between 1933 and 1945.

In order to fulfill these tasks, *Die Deutsche Bibliothek* has the right by law to require submission of the "legal depository copy" (*Pflichtexemplarrecht*) for the Federal Republic of Germany. This law makes it mandatory for each publisher to deliver two copies of each new publication – whether it is a publication in paper form, microform, sound recording, audiovisual media or an electronic publication. The legal requirements are specified by the legal depository copy ordinance (*Pflichtstückverordnung*) and the collection guidelines. The clearly defined legal charge to collect these items makes *Die Deutsche Bibliothek* into a universal library for the German language area, that is, it collects and cata-

Statistics on the National Universal Libraries and the Central Subject Libraries for 2002

Library Name	Collection No. of volumes	Expenditures for Acquisitions and Binding (in Euros)	Local Circulation Transactions	Interlibrary Loans / Document Deliveries
Berlin SBB	9,872,000	10,617,400	1,466,731	78,852
Frankfurt/M DDB	5,676,000	1,024,000	456,586	13,964
Hanover TIB	5,600,000	6,900,000	674,400	428,000
Kiel IfW/ZBW	2,608,000	1,250,000	120,559	55,100
Cologne ZBMed	1,200,000	3,842,400	130,214	526,297
Leipzig DDB	8,338,000	715,500	381,688	4,245
Munich BSB	7,822,000	10,861,000	1,173,442	43,534

The new building of *Die Deutsche Bibliothek in Frankfurt/Main* (Hesse) (architects: Arat, Kaiser, Kaiser), took over six years to build and was dedicated in 1997. Its main usage space comprises 77,000 sqm, and it offers space for 18 million publications. If the an expected daily increase of 1,000 titles continues, the capacity of this building will last until the year 2035. A reading area (3,200 sqm) with 350 work spaces and a reference library of 100,000 volumes is available for library patrons.

logs literature from all areas of knowledge. Due to its archival function, *Die Deutsche Bibliothek* does not lend these items, but offers its collections to the public for onsite use.

Die Deutsche Bibliothek is not only the central archival library and the central music archives for the Federal Republic of Germany, but also the national bibliographic center. It fulfills this part of its task by the compilation and publication of the *German National Bibliography (Deutsche Nationalbibliographie – DNB)*, which is divided into several series. The bibliographic cataloging record is also the basis for various central services which external users and customers can take advantage of – not only in Germany. Data from the *German National Bibliography* can be purchased on different information media, from the printed catalog card via the diskette and CD-ROM up to the online database BIBLIODATA and the copy cataloging services from the FTP or WWW server and is available in the data formats MAB, USMARC or UNIMARC. With the assistance of the CIP-Service (Cataloguing in Publication), to which approximately 5,500 publishers participate with 50,000 titles per year, *Die Deutsche Bibliothek* has informed both the book trade and the libraries promptly about new publications since 1974. As of 2003, a "New Publications Service" (*Neuerscheinungsdienst*) which is a joint cooperative venture of *Die Deutsche Bibliothek* together with the Book Sellers Association (*Buchhändler-Vereinigung*), which publishes the *German Books In Print* (*Verzeichnis Lieferbarer Bücher* – VLB) in printed and in digital form, has taken over this task.

Die Deutsche Bibliothek devotes special attention to the documentation of the German-language authors in emigration and exile during the years of the National Socialist regime from 1933–1945. The Collection of Exile Literature (*Sammlung Exil-Literatur*) of the *Deutsche Bücherei* in Leipzig and the German Exile Archive (*Deutsches Exilarchiv*) of *Die Deutsche Bibliothek* in Frankfurt am Main contain published books, brochures, and journals of the German emigrants abroad, as well as the personal records of individual emigrants and the archives of exile organizations.

Die Deutsche Bücherei in Leipzig houses an international research library of documentation on the Holocaust. The *Anne Frank Shoah Library* (Leipzig) pursues the goal of making available all literature published worldwide on the persecution and destruction of European Jews by the National Socialist government in Germany. Publications on other peoples and groups who were persecuted because of ethnical, political, religious or other reasons, also fall into this collection emphasis.

The German Book and Writing Museum (*Das Deutsche Buch- und Schriftmuseum*) in the *Deutsche Bücherei* in Leipzig is a documentation center for the history and culture of the book. In a time when audiovisual and electronic media come into greater competition with the book, the preservation of valuable examples of the book and writing

The German Music Archives (*Deutsches Musikarchiv* – DMA) in Berlin was founded in 1970 and is integrated into *Die Deutsche Bibliothek* in Frankfurt am Main as a department. It is the central collection point for sheet music and musical recordings, as well as being Germany's bibliographic information center for musical works. In 1978, the DMA moved into the „Herrenhaus Correns" (also known as the „Siemens Villa") in Berlin-Lankwitz and currently owns around 957,000 media units.

culture are gaining in significance. Founded in 1884 – which makes it the oldest book museum in the world – this Museum presents its extensive and valuable collections, including the largest collection of watermarked papers in the world, to a wide audience in both special and permanent exhibitions.

The Center for Book Conservation (*Zentrum für Bucherhaltung*) in Leipzig was part of the *Deutsche Bücherei* until 1998 and has since then become an independent corporation that is concerned with the conservation and restoration of books as physical objects. Tens of thousands of books, for which the raw materials were not based on textiles (rags) but rather were created from the basis of wood pulp, have been threatened by acid deterioration since the middle of the 19th century. With methods of treatment both using machines and by hand, the endangered pages are made stiff through the so-called *paper-splitting* technique and preserved through deacidification. Microfilming also preserves the texts of the endangered books.

In its function as national library, *Die Deutsche Bibliothek* cooperates with national and international library institutions. It participates in numerous national and international projects. As examples, the following are named here: compilation of common rules, standards and norms, the cooperative leadership for creating authority file databases, the development of strategies and methods for mass deacidification, the definition of a metadata standard for indexing digital and digitized resources, and the function of a national ISSN center for Germany.

The basic restriction of the mission of *Die Deutsche Bibliothek* to collect and care for German-language literature distinguishes it from the national libraries of many other countries which also acquire the most important foreign or foreign-language publications on their country and thereby often become large universal libraries with a considerable collection of national and foreign literature. This second part of the task of a national library is fulfilled in Germany primarily by two very important universal libraries: the State Library in Berlin – Prussian Cultural Heritage Foundation (*Staatsbibliothek zu Berlin – Preußischer Kulturbesitz*) (founded in 1661) and the Bavarian State Library (*Bayerische Staatsbibliothek*) in Munich (founded in 1558). Both have evolved from court libraries of princes, and both carry out supraregional (national) functions due to their excellent collections and numerous services. With their comprehensive German and international older collections, their numerous special collections, and their participation in the Special Subject Collection Program of the DFG, as well as in the Consortium of Collections of German Printed Materials, they can be designated as the central or national universal libraries. For the applied sciences, they are augmented by the three Central Subject Libraries, in the area of German national literature through the other libraries of the Consortium for the Collection of German Printed Materials (*Arbeitsgemeinschaft Sammlung Deutscher Drucke*).

The State Library of Berlin – Prussian Cultural Heritage (Staatsbibliothek zu Berlin – Preußischer Kulturbesitz)

The State Library of Berlin – Prussian Cultural Heritage (*Staatsbibliothek zu Berlin – Preußischer Kulturbesitz* – SBB-PK) continues the tradition of the Prussian State Library, which was one of the largest and most important scholarly universal libraries of Europe before the Second World War. Its successful development met an abrupt end through the effects of the War and the division of Germany. The separate development of the German State Library (*Deutsche Staatsbibliothek*), which had shared the tasks of a "national library" for the territory of the GDR together with the *Deutsche Bücherei* in Leipzig, and the State Library of the Prussian Cultural Heritage (*Staatsbibliothek Preußischer Kulturbesitz*), which had grown out of the former collections of the Prussian State Library that had remained in the West after the War, could finally be ended with the reunification of Germany.

In 1978, 33 years after the end of the Second World War, the State Library Prussian Cultural Heritage could finally unite its collections and move into a new building on Potsdamer Platz in Berlin-Tiergarten (architect: Hans Scharoun), the current Building 2 of the State Library of Berlin – Prussian Cultural Heritage (*Haus 2 der Staatsbibliothek zu Berlin – Preußischer Kulturbesitz*). It functions as a lending and a functional workplace library, as well as an information center, while Building 1 is organized as a reference and research library only.

In both buildings on the boulevard "Unter den Linden" (Building 1) and at "Potsdamer Platz" (Building 2), the State Library is making the attempt to re-establish its former ranking as an excellent research library in reunified Berlin, and to take on central functions for German librarianship.

The State Library possesses an impressive collection of printed works. Almost ten million books and journals from all areas of knowledge, countries, periods and languages are available for research.

Areas of emphasis have been formed for literature treating East Europe, East Asia and the Orient, official publications and parliamentary papers, the publications of international organizations, journals, and newspapers, as well as children's and youth literature. With 2.3 million microfiches and microfilms, the State Library is well represented in the area of microforms. Of particularly prominent significance are the special collections. Of them, the following special collections deserve special mention: the oriental manuscripts (including 18,300 manuscripts and 320,000 hand-written authors' manuscripts (Autographen), the musicology collection (including 450,000 items of sheet music, 66,000 hand-written musical scores), cartographic works (including 940,000 pages of maps) and oriental studies (41,000 manuscripts). With a collection breadth surpassing many others, the image archive has 13.5 million photographs, graphic illustrations, engravings, slides and other pictorial representations.

Within the system of national literature and information provision, the State Library takes on many responsibilities. In context of the program for national literature provision financed by the German Research Council (Deutsche Forschungsgemeinschaft – DFG), it maintains several special subject areas, including law and jurisprudence. In the cooperative acquisitions program, the Collection of German Imprints (Sammlung Deutscher Drucke), the State Library is responsible for the publication years 1871–1912. It also collects German and foreign official publications and the publications of international organizations.

With its bibliographic services, the State Library has a connecting link with the corresponding activities of the Prussian State Library. It produces the international Union Catalog of Incunabula, maintains the central catalog of the hand-written author manuscripts (Autographen), which electronically administers 1.2 million hand-written documents, participates in several other cataloging and classification projects, for example for the German imprints of the 16th and 17th century, and it maintains the library work for the German Periodicals Database (Zeitschriftendatenbank). Finally, it must be mentioned that the State Library of Berlin runs the international ISBN Agency and the international ISMN agency, both of which serve the worldwide distribution of the standard numbering system for books and for musical publications.

The Bavarian State Library in Munich

With around 7.6 million volumes of national and international literature, the Bavarian State Library (Bayerische Staatsbibliothek – BSB) in Munich is the second largest scholarly universal library in the Federal Republic of Germany and owns one of the most significant collections of primary sources in the world. At the same time, it is the central state library (Landesbibliothek) of the Free State of Bavaria and the state service center for public libraries in all areas concerning Bavarian librarianship; since 1663, it has collected the legal depository copies of all works published in Bavaria. With its more than 40,600 journals and newspaper subscriptions, it is

The Bavarian State Library (Bayerische Staatsbibliothek – BSB) in Munich was first given its own building in 1843, built according to the plans of Friedrich von Gärtner. Since its building process and conception followed functional aspects, it was considered the best German library building at the time of its completion. With its monumental staircase in the interior, it also succeeded in achieving a representational effect. The limited storage area forced the BSB, as is the case with many other German libraries, to store a large part of its collection in remote storage.

the largest periodicals library in Europe after the British Library.

Founded in 1558 as the court library of the House of Wittelsbach, this library has used its present name, the Bavarian State Library, since 1919. It collects publications of all countries and subject areas. Special areas of focus include studies of antiquity and archaeology, history, music, East and Southeast Europe, and the Orient and East Asia. Because of its tradition and development, a special area of collection emphasis is on manuscripts and imprints before 1700, as well as foreign literature of the post-World War II era.

With 84,000 manuscripts, the manuscript collection is the largest in the world. Just as meaningful is the collection of early imprints (incunabula) numbering 18,664 volumes. Since the Bavarian State Library has also attained a top position in the collection of 16th and 17th century imprints from the German-language area, it took on the leadership for the corresponding national bibliographic cataloging projects, as well as for the Collection of German Imprints (*Sammlung Deutscher Drucke*) (for the time period 1450 to 1600, sheet music imprints up to 1800). In context of the Special Subject Area Collection Project of the German Research Foundation (*Deutsche Forschungsgemeinschaft*), the Bavarian State Library has taken on several special subject collection areas. The international orientation in its collection development practices can be easily seen in the fact that four-fifths of all of its book acquisitions have originated on foreign soil.

Similar to the State Library of Berlin, the Bavarian State Library in Munich also participates in numerous national and international cooperative projects. It maintains partnerships with international associations and foreign libraries. Proceeding from the insight that the heritage of the past is based on the book, that the book will also play a leading role in the future, but that the electronic media will open totally new possibilities, the efforts of the Library are directed towards the preservation of the older collections on the one hand, and on the other hand, towards the establishment of modern technology. The Bavarian State Library thus supports both the Institute for Book and Manuscript Restoration (*Institut für Buch- und Handschriftenrestaurierung*) and also the Munich Digitalization Center (*Münchener Digitalisierungszentrum – MDZ*).

The German Central Library of Medicine (*Deutsche Zentralbibliothek für Medizin*) in Cologne (North Rhine-Westphalia), the predecessors of which can be traced to the year 1908, is one of the largest special libraries for medicine in the world. The Library lies in the middle of the Cologne University Clinic. In the Clinic building shown here, the Library occupies several stories. A reading room and a textbook collection are available for onsite use.

The Central Subject Libraries

The three *Central Subject Libraries* (*Zentrale Fachbibliotheken*) in Hanover, Cologne and Kiel serve supraregional (national) literature provision in the applied sciences. In their respective subject areas, they supplement *Die Deutsche Bibliothek* and the two central universal libraries (State Libraries) in Berlin and Munich in fulfilling national tasks by maintaining a breadth and depth of the collection. It collects publications in the assigned subject area with the greatest possible completeness, including non-conventional literature and non-book media of all kinds, and makes these available for interlibrary loan and document delivery. For this reason, it receives joint funding from the Federal Government and the *Länder*.

The Technical Information Library (*Technische Informationsbibliothek* – TIB) in Hanover, founded in 1959, is the German central subject library for all areas of technology and the basic sciences associated with them, especially chemistry, computer science, mathematics, and physics. It sees its primary task as the differentiated, customized document delivery service passed on to the user needs and provided in the shortest possible time. The prerequisite for this is comprehensive acquisition and archiving of technical and scientific literature – both conventional and "grey" literature (outside the book trade) – from the entire world. With 18,600 current professional journal subscriptions and five million volumes, microforms and CD-ROMs, including conference proceedings, research reports, patent papers, norms, standards and dissertations, the Library fulfills its extensive tasks.

The German Central Library of Medicine (*Deutsche Zentralbibliothek für Medizin* – ZB-Med) in Cologne, founded in 1969, is the central subject library for human medicine and its fundamental supporting areas of science. With 650,000 volumes, 430,000 dissertations and 9,000 current periodicals, it is the largest medical library in Europe. In addition to the online catalog for its own collections, and a current contents database for journal tables of contents, it offers its patrons access to over 2,000 electronic journals. Its work is supplemented by the German Institute for Medical Documentation and Information (*Deutsches Institut für Medizinische Dokumentation und Information* – DIMDI) – also located in Cologne – which prepares and offers online medical databases. Since 2001, the ZB-Med maintains a branch library in Bonn focussing on the special subject areas of nutrition and the environment (which include partial collections of the former German Central Subject Library for Agriculture).

The German Central Library for Economics (*Deutsche Zentralbibliothek für Wirtschaftswissenschaften)* in Kiel, along with the Library of the Insti-

tute for World Economies (*Institut für Weltwirtschaft* – IfW), which was founded as a departmental library in 1914, is the largest special library for economics in the world. It possesses 2.6 million volumes, including working papers, reports, statistics, dissertations and conference proceedings, and subscribes to 16,000 print and electronic journals. Their collections concentrate on the larger areas of political economy and world economy, and specifically include the publications of international organizations. As a rule, literature from all countries of the world and in all languages is collected. The online catalog ECONIS, based on 1.2 million titles, has articles from journals and books indexed and classified according to the standard thesaurus *Thesaurus Wirtschaft* ("Economics Thesaurus"). Collections are provided to the library users via interlibrary loan and via electronic ordering and document delivery services.

State Libraries (*Landesbibliotheken*) and other Regional Libraries

The approximately 40 State (*Landesbibliotheken*) and other regional libraries serve the literature provision in a certain region which either stretches over an entire Federal state (*Land*) or a part of a Federal state, a governing partition, a county or a city with its surroundings; a state or regional library does not serve the literature provision of an institution of higher education or other institution. In terms of their origins, their size, the consolidation of their collections, their funding bodies, and especially

The State Library of Oldenburg (*Landesbibliothek Oldenburg*) (Lower Saxony), a scholarly universal library with regional area of emphasis, was founded in 1792. In 1987 it was given its present accommodations in a reconstructed and expanded infantry barracks. Its collection of 650,000 media units are also used by members of the University of Oldenburg which opened 1974.

The Lower Saxony State Library (*Niedersächsische Landesbibliothek)* in Hanover (Lower Saxony) owns the significant *Nachlass* of Gottfried Wilhelm Leibniz; it is also a center for producing an edition of the works of this universal scholar. Among the items in the *Nachlass* is Leibniz' *calculating machine* from 1695, which functions for all four basic arithmetic calculations. The decisive constructional elements of this machine have remained valid into the 20ᵗʰ century.

their name, these regional libraries differ greatly from one another and thus form an apparently heterogeneously composed group. However, since they fundamentally have the same functions, they fall into the same category or library type. Even though they refer to purely state libraries or regional libraries, most often – but by no means always – they carry the name *Landesbibliothek* ("state library" – referring to the *Länder* level or state) or *Staatliche Bibliothek* ("State Library" – referring to the Federal level or State).

Taking the exceptions into consideration, the regional libraries (*Regionalbibliotheken*) have a more clearly defined universal collection policy – even if many libraries have their areas of emphasis in the humanities and social sciences subjects because of their history. Therefore it is possible for them to cover literature needs for scholarly uses and other literature information for the population in their area of territorial responsibility – be it a city, a region or an entire state (*Bundesland*). Their particular obligation, however, lies with the task of complete acquisition, archiving, cataloguing and indexing, and making the literature of the region itself available. While *Die Deutsche Bibliothek* has the legal depository copy for the entire Federal Republic of Germany, libraries with regional functions also

have legal depository rights for their region or for their state (*Bundesland*).

The depository copy law, which most regional libraries take advantage of, is the basis for the production and current publication of a bibliography of all publications produced in that state (*Land*), the purpose of which consists of providing bibliographic references for all new publications on a *Land*, its regions and communities and all persons associated with the *Land*. Up to now, this has taken place in the form of a printed bibliography, but now the database format, which allows searching via the Internet, is slowly replacing the book form. State bibliographies (*Landesbibliographien*) now cover publications of the entire Federal Republic of Germany.

The cataloging and maintenance of traditionally processed older holdings, the collection and processing of personal records and archives of famous persons of state, the preservation of literary archives, and an intensive cultural and public relations program with exhibitions, lectures, readings, concerts, etc., are additional typical tasks of *Landesbibliotheken* and *Regionalbibliotheken*. To achieve this, they are often supported by library societies

The State and City Library of Augsburg (*Staats- und Stadtbibliothek Augsburg*) (Bavaria), founded in 1537, represents the library type of *scholarly city library*; for the region under the Swabian government, it takes advantage of depository copy legislation and fulfills the tasks of an archive and a regional library. The neo-Baroque building with its self-supporting bookshelves in the lower storage area was already considered exemplary in the year marking its construction, 1893.

and Friends of the Library groups which assist through member contributions and donations they have collected, especially when the library budget does not allow such activities or when unconventional action is necessary.

Most state libraries (*Landesbibliotheken*) have evolved from court libraries; some of them owe their existence to the function of having been a storage library for the items taken from monasteries during the Secularization (Amberg, Bamberg, Passau, Regensburg); others have collections which are historically bound up closely with the *Gymnasium libraries* (Coburg, Gotha); only a few were first founded in the 20th century by the Federal Government or by another political subdivision (Aurich, Koblenz, Speyer). The *scholarly city libraries* (*Wissenschaftliche Stadtbibliotheken*), which have evolved from *city council libraries* (*Ratsbüchereien*) or from *historical city libraries* (Lübeck, Nürnberg, Ulm) were once present in Germany in large numbers but their numbers have since decreased; some (Berlin, Dortmund) have only been established in the 20th century; others can be traced back to university libraries which have since been dissolved (Mainz, Trier).

For historical and geographical reasons, several Federal states in Germany have more than one older *Landesbibliothek* which developed as a result of the distinct historical-political territories; other smaller states do not have even one *Landesbibliothek*. In these cases, the university libraries in that area take over the regional functions additionally to their own tasks of serving the educational institution, and this double function is also indicated in their name. Thus, we find the designations "University and State Library" (*Universitäts- und Landesbibliothek*) (Bonn, Düsseldorf, Halle, Jena, Münster, Saarbrücken), "State and University Library" (*Staats- und Universitätsbibliothek*) (Bremen, Hamburg) or "State and College Library" (*Landes- und Hochschulbibliothek*) (Darmstadt) or "College and State Library" (*Hochschul- und Landesbibliothek*) (Fulda).

On the other hand, regional libraries take part in the literature provision for study, research, and teaching. They are integrated in the regional and supraregional (nation-wide) structures of academic and research librarianship, make their scholarly literature available through interlibrary loan, and are particularly interesting for research purposes be-

cause of their older and special collections. Especially in the cities with newly-founded universities (Augsburg, Bamberg, Trier) or other institutions of higher education (Zwickau), as well as in cities where universities have grown out of technical colleges (Karlsruhe, Stuttgart), the regional libraries take on subsidiary functions for provision of literature at the university for certain subject areas. In Hanover, a special relationship exists between the University Library and the Lower Saxony *Landesbibliothek* which is regulated through a service contract.

Several of the former courtly libraries with valuable historical book collections have specialized in selected areas of the humanities and cultural history and consider themselves today as *research libraries* (*Forschungsbibliotheken*) with a completely individual profile. The orientation to research outside of the universities is expressed in the independent scholarly activity of the library and in the support of research through the editorial preparation of literary editions, awarding of scholarships, preparing and hosting of international conferences. The *Duke August Library* (*Herzog August Bibliothek*) in Wölfenbüttel belongs to this group which

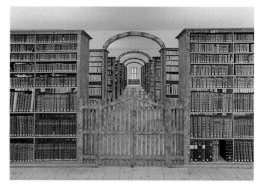

The Library of the Francke Foundations (*Bibliothek der Franckeschen Stiftungen*) in Halle (Saxony-Anhalt), established in 1698 in connection with the founding of an orphanage, has had its own library building since 1728. The collections were held in shelves arranged in this room as if they were theatre backdrops. After restoration was completed in 1998, the Baroque "back-drop" library (*"Kulissenbibliothek"*) could be presented again its in original, 18th century appearance.

specializes in European cultural history of early modern times, as does also the *Duchess Anna Amalia Library* (*Herzogin Anna Amalia Bibliothek*) in Weimar, which dedicates itself intensively to German language works from the Classical Period. Both libraries have excellent older collections which are shelved in open access stacks for researchers and arranged to a great extent according to a systematic classification scheme. In addition, they also acquire the corresponding current secondary literature.

The *Research Library of Gotha* (*Forschungsbibliothek Gotha*), which is organizationally connected to the University Library of Erfurt, holds a comprehensive older collection, originally oriented to all fields of scholarship, but since 1850 dominated by the humanities. The *Main Library of the Francke Foundations* (*Hauptbibliothek der Franckeschen Stiftungen*) in Halle cannot be traced back to a previous regional library, but was rather established for educational purposes in 1698. It is considered a research library for the areas of ecclesiastical history and the history of education in the early modern times, and correspondingly has focal areas for these fields in its collection policy.

Libraries of Higher Education Institutions

In the Federal Republic of Gemany, the funding of institutions of higher education is usually the responsibility of the Federal states (*Bundesländer*). The three-tiered division of the various institutions of higher education is also the basis of division for the libraries of these higher education institutions.

Including the departmental libraries, there are almost 3,600 libraries of very different sizes at the approximately 250 institutions of higher education. Together, they offer the 1.9 million students about 157 million books and 534,000 current periodicals. The acquisitions budgets total just under 400 million DM = 202 million Euros (DBS 2002).

Libraries of Universities

The libraries of the 79 universities and other institutions of higher education at the same level primarily serve the literature provision of the university community members from students to professors in supporting study, research, and teaching. Thus they

The Library of the *Historicum*, a departmental library (*Teilbibliothek*) of the University Library in Munich (*Universitätsbibliothek München*) (Bavaria), has combined the collections which were previously kept in separate departmental libraries and since its opening in 1999 these collections are now under one roof. It offers the 2,700 students and 180 instructors of history, archaeology, and Byzantine studies 325 reading places and a reference collection of 240,000 volumes.

functionally form a homogenous group – even though they are in part considerably different from each other in terms of their age and their historical development in the size of their collection, the number of users, the size of the budget, etc. All university libraries can also be used for scholarly purposes by non-university members; some have even expressly taken on further regional functions. In addition to the traditional literature provision through their own collections, these libraries have offered information reference services for quite some time, as well as databases and electronic publications in context of the "digital library" (*Digitale Bibliothek*).

Most university libraries offer their users between 1.5 and 2.5 million volumes. Many older university libraries (Freiburg, Heidelberg, Jena, Tübingen), as well as the State and University Library Hamburg (*Staats- und Universitätsbibliothek Hamburg*), founded after the Second World War, the University and City Library of Cologne (*Universitäts- und Stadtbibliothek Köln*) rechartered in 1919, and individual libraries emerging in the 1960's (Bremen, Düsseldorf, Regensburg), have collections numbering between 2.5 and 3 million volumes. The group of the largest libraries with collections of between 3 to 4 million volumes include the Library of the *Humboldt University of Berlin*, the City and University Library in Frankfurt am Main (*Stadt- und Universitätsbibliothek Frankfurt am Main*) with the natural sciences collections of the *Senckenberg Library*, and the State and University Library of Göttingen (*Staats- und Universitätsbibliothek Göttingen*). The libraries of the smaller institutions of higher education, especially those with more restricted course offerings, lie significantly under the 1 million volume level (Hildesheim, Koblenz/Landau, Lübeck). The number of current periodical subscriptions of most of the university libraries varies between 5,000 to 10,000 titles. In addition to printed journals, there are increasing subscriptions to electronic journals. These are offered in context of virtual serials libraries to the members of the university community.

Fundamentally, university libraries have responsibility for collecting works of all areas of scholarship, that is, they must also take subjects into consideration in their collection development policy which are not taught at that particular institution. Since the 1960's, libraries have built up textbook collections to support the students with current textbooks for their study. A large number of university libraries have taken on a Special Subject Collection Area or even several, and make the literature acquired through the financial assistance of the DFG available for supraregional use through the interlibrary loan network. Just as important as the new acquisitions are the older and special collections which the older universities have at their disposal and which is often reflected in their names (often those of their founders). Many of these older and

At the oldest university of Germany in *Heidelberg* (Baden-Württemberg), founded in 1386, a two-layered library system exists with a central *University Library* (*Universitätsbibliothek*) and over 100 departmental libraries. Among the worlds renowned Cimelia of the Library is the "Large Heidelberg Song Manuscript" (*„Große Heidelberger Liederhandschrift"*), the *Codex Manesse*, with the popular miniature of Walther von der Vogelweide (*Cod. Pal. germ.* 848, *Fol.* 124r).

special collections include manuscripts, hand-written authors' manuscripts, *Nachlässe*, early imprints, maps, musical scores, and many others. The technical university libraries possess standards and patent papers which make their collections valuable for these special types of literature.

Two basic forms in the university library structure in Germany can be distinguished: these are most often designated as "*single-layered*" ("*einschichtig*") and "*two-layered*" ("*zweischichtig*") library systems.

At traditional universities with the *two-layered library system,* the central university library has a closed stacks storage area and a lending area, a textbook collection, and user services, such as inter-library loan and information reference services. The second layer is comprised of a large number of in-dependent departmental, institute, or faculty librar-ies which are usually non-lending reference libraries with arrangement of the books according to a clas-sification scheme on open access stacks. While the central university library acquires the general, inter-disciplinary literature, the departmental libraries – which have their own budgets – concentrate on the literature of their subject area, especially highly specialized research literature. To reduce the disad-vantages of this dualism and to strengthen the measures taken since the recommendations for co-operation given by the German Research Founda-tion, cooperative library systems have emerged at many universities. However, even where the reform of university laws has made the director in charge of all staff within the library system and has pre-scribed a standard library system, the practical implementation of the so-called functional single-layered-ness in a previously two-layered system re-mains a difficult task. The exorbitant price increases for journal subscriptions, the availability and man-agement of electronic resources, and the employ-ment of professionally qualified staff are factors which are favorable for the currently observed ten-dencies towards centralization.

At the new universities which have been foun-ded since the late Sixties and most of which have a *single-layered library system*, there is only one li-brary which takes on both functions of a central university library and of the decentralized depart-mental libraries. This unified library structure was also introduced in the universities of the GDR and has been continued after reunification, but because of the continuous construction problems it has not been realized in all libraries. Single-layered library systems are characterized by a single director with professional supervision and authority to give direc-tions to the entire library staff, and by the central allocation and distribution of the acquisitions bud-get. Most of the library work procedures are cen-tralized. The collections – partially allowed to be cir-culated, partially only for reference and onsite use – are often spread among several departmental li-braries, but occasionally also concentrated at one location; in any case, they are always shelved in open access areas according to a finely detailed classification system.

Libraries of the Universities of Applied Science and other Higher Educational Institutions

The German technical colleges, some of which are now universities of applied science, form a relatively new type of higher educational institution – in the Western German States since the 1970's, in the Eastern States only after 1990. They have grown out of former engineering schools and higher tech-nical colleges for economics, social work, design and other subject areas. In contrast to the universi-ties, the universities of applied science and techni-cal colleges do not have the objective of transmit-ting a scientific (theoretical) education to the stu-dents; instead they enable the students to carry out independent activities in their profession transmit-ted through practice-oriented instruction based on a scientific experience.

Therefore, in contrast to the university libraries, the approximately 156 libraries of the universities of applied science and technical colleges are not uni-versal in scope, but rather special libraries which concentrate on the subject areas taught in their in-stitutions. According to the educational mission of the universities of applied science described above, these libraries contain basic literature and text-books, often in large numbers. The size of these libraries differs greatly. In some cases, several insti-tutions of higher education have been united in *one* university of applied sciences which has a li-brary of over 250,000 volumes and subscribes to up to 1,000 periodicals. In other cases, however, considerably smaller universities of applied science and technical colleges with limited course offerings have libraries of a modest size.

The libraries of the art and music academies are – corresponding to the lesser significance of litera-ture in the musical and artistic courses of study – comparably small; an absolute exception is the Li-brary of the Academy of the Fine Arts (*Hochschule der Künste*) in Berlin (280,000 volumes). Libraries are also maintained by administrative academies (public administration colleges), the established professional academies in some states (*Bundes-länder*) and in higher educational institutions with private funding agencies. Only in Baden-Württem-berg are there still independent teachers' colleges with corresponding libraries; in the rest of the Fed-eral states, teacher education is integrated into the

The German Central Library for Economics (*Deutsche Zentralbibliothek für Wirtschaftswissenschaften*) in Kiel (Schleswig-*Holstein*), with 2.6 million volumes the world's largest special library for business and economics literature, moved into a building extension in 2001 with 6,400 sqm of usable space (architect: Walter von Lom). Together with the older building of the Institute for World Economy (*Institut für Weltwirtschaft*), constructed at the turn of the century, the former guest house of the Krupp Family, an impressive building complex emerged on the banks of the Kiel Fjord which joined together research departments, library, and closed book storage stacks.

university, or the teachers' college has been expanded to a university.

Special Libraries and Technical Libraries

The largest and at the same time itself a very heterogeneous group of scholarly libraries is formed by the approximately 2,700 special libraries, which include those of public, religious, and private institutions. The common aspect of these libraries is the restriction to a specific subject area and the connection to an institution for which the library is exclusively (or at least primarily) responsible to for providing the needed literature. The acquisition of new literature in special libraries is totally directed to the current and practical needs of the employees of the specific institution and specifically considers works which appear outside the normal commercial book trade. Much more important than books are print and electronic journals in special and technical libraries. Particularly in the special libraries devoted to the natural sciences and technology, use of online information is increasingly replacing the traditional form of literature provision; some corporate libraries already exclusively or primarily subscribe to electronic information resources. Cataloging and indexing often extends beyond the bibliographic and subject cataloging that is carried out in the academic universal libraries; it encompasses an intensive documentation activity and includes individual, user-customized services. Special libraries are generally reference libraries, although many of them participate in the German interlibrary loan network. Since they usually work for a limited clientele, whose information needs and literature wishes are known, the service orientation is especially pronounced in special libraries.

Within the large number of special libraries, the over 500 parliamentary, administrative and judicial libraries (*Parlaments-, Behörden und Gerichtsbibliotheken*) form a very homogenous group. These institutions, most of which only came into being after 1945, serve the primary objectives of the administration and jurisdiction, and are therefore specialized in the acquisition of legal and political literature. Official publications, government documents, and "grey literature" (*Graues Schrifttum*) constitute a large part of these collections. These, too, are libraries for onsite use only and allow public use only under very limited conditions or even not at all.

In addition to the already mentioned Library of the German Parliament and the libraries of the parliaments and governments of the *Länder*, the libraries of the ministries and the supreme Federal administrative offices must also be mentioned. Individually, they can have a very respectable size, as is evidenced by the Senate Library (*Senatsbibliothek*) in Berlin (482,000 volumes), the Library of the Foreign Ministry Office (*Auswärtiges Amt*) in Berlin (290,000 volumes, 91,000 maps and atlases), the

German Patent Office (*Deutsches Patentamt*) in Munich (895,000 volumes including the patents themselves, 37 million patent documents) and the Federal Office of Statistics (*Statistisches Bundesamt*) in Wiesbaden (440,000 volumes).

Among the libraries of the courts of the *Länder* and the Federal Government, especially those of the Federal Supreme Court (*Bundesgerichtshofs*) (490,000 volumes) and of the Federal Constitutional Court (*Bundesverfassungsgerichts*) (330,000 volumes), both of which are located in Karlsruhe, are pre-eminent. As in all special libraries, other literature and media forms play an important role in the judicial libraries (besides books and journals, there are many microforms and electronic media); the Library of the Federal Constitutional Court, for instance, maintains an archive that contains 1.1 million indexed press clippings.

The category of *special libraries* in a narrow sense includes the libraries of Federal Government research institutes and the *Länder* research institutions, of scientific societies, as well as archives, museums and clinics. In addition, it includes libraries

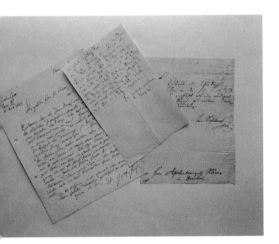

Autographen (hand-written authors' manuscripts) are traditionally collected by many academic and research libraries. This illustration shows the letters of the writers Friedrich Schiller, Franz Kafka, and Günter Grass from the collection of the German Literary Archive (*Deutsches Literaturarchiv*) in Marbach on the Neckar River (Baden-Württemberg). Together with the Schiller National Museum, it pursues the goal of collecting all texts and documents referring to German literature. The Marbach institutions are archives, library, and museum all in one.

belonging to religious corporate bodies and institutions, including the monasteries, but also those maintained by companies, federations, associations, and societies. Even with the vast differentiation in the individual cases, one can still see that special libraries concentrate their collection directives on very specific literature and usually purchase a high percentage of "grey" and non-conventional literature. These libraries use electronically available resources intensively, carry out indepth cataloging of parts of other works (articles, book chapters, etc.), maintain their collections as reference collections, and abstain from permanently archiving old titles which are no longer being used. The comprehensiveness of their collections differs incredibly and ranges from well over 1 million volumes down to a few thousand titles. Correspondingly, the number of staff varies, and many special libraries can be best characterized as "*One Person Libraries*" (OPL).

From the broad spectrum of special libraries, comprising all different disciplines, we can only give a few examples here. There are many special libraries in the field of pure and applied science and technology, e.g. the Library of the German Science Museum (*Deutsches Museum*) in Munich, a special library for science, technology and their history (850,000 volumes), the *Kekulè-Bibliothek* of Bayer AG, a large chemical and pharmaceutical company in Leverkusen (650,000 volumes), the central library of the Research Center Jülich (*Forschungszentrum Jülich GmbH*), specializing in modern technology (400,000 volumes, 280,000 reports), and the library of the German Academy of Researchers in the Natural Sciences (*Deutsche Akademie der Naturforscher Leopoldina*) in Halle (250,000 volumes). For the area of medicine, two representative libraries are the central library of German Cancer Research Center (*Deutsches Krebsforschungszentrum*) in Heidelberg (80,000 media units) and the Physicians' Central Library of the University Clinic (*Ärztliche Zentralbibliothek des Universitäts-Klinikums*) at Hamburg-Eppendorf (262,000 media units).

In the humanities, which are particularly dependant on literature, special libraries play an additional, important role in their support of research outside the universities. Some examples are: The Library of the Friedrich Ebert Foundation (*Friedrich-Ebert-Stiftung*) in Bonn, which as a foundation associated with a political party, specializes in the his-

tory of the Social Democrat party of Germany and of the labor movements (550,000 volumes); the Library of the *Ibero-Amerikanisches Instituts* in Berlin (765,000 volumes), the Library of the German National Museum (*Germanisches Nationalmuseum*) in Nuremberg, where the collections cover the history of art and culture (570,000 volumes), the Library of the Research Office for Military History (*Bibliothek des Militärgeschichtlichen Forschungsamtes*) in Potsdam (240,000 media units). Special mention should be given to the German Literary Archives (*Deutsches Literaturarchiv)* in Marbach on the Neckar River, which as library and archive together functions as the collection point for German literature and the literary tradition in the German language from the times of Enlightenment to the present (760,000 volumes, 1,100 authors' bequests, 200,000 images).

In the areas of religion and theology, naturally the ecclesiastical special libraries funded by the churches are predominant. They support scholarly research, and often serve both ecclesiastical administration and the theological seminaries. Among them, supported by the Catholic Church are, for example, the monastic libraries (*Benediktinerabtei Beuron*, 400,000 volumes) and the diocesan libraries (*Erzbischöfliche Diözesan- and Dombibliothek* at Cologne, 410,000 volumes, over 1,100 current

The *Johannes a Lasco Bibliothek* (Lower Saxony), oldest Library in East Friesland, grew out of the Library of the reformed Protestant Congregation of Emden, founded in 1559. Since 1993, it has been named after the Polish reformer Jan Laski, Superintendent of the entire East Friesian Church. In 1995, the library was moved into the renovated "Large Church" ("*Große Kirche*") in Emden. As a scholarly special library, research center, and cultural center, it has supraregional significance. In 2001, it was selected by the DBV as the "Library of the Year" ("*Bibliothek des Jahres*").

periodicals), and supported by the Protestant Church are, for example, the libraries of the regional congregations (*Landeskirchen*) e.g., (*Nordelbische Kirchenbibliothek* in Hamburg, 180,000 volumes). Owned by an ecclesiastical foundation of civil law, the *Johannes a Lasco Bibliothek* in Emden (90,000 volumes) is a special library for reformed Protestantism (Calvinism) and ecclesiastical history of early modern times.

In political sciences, law, and economics, the parliamentary, administrative and judicial (court) libraries, mentioned already, take on a significant meaning. In addition to those, six of the *Max Planck Institutes* specialize in particular branches of law and maintain respective special libraries; these are in Freiburg (280,000 volumes), Frankfurt/Main (230,000 volumes), Hamburg (350,000 volumes), Heidelberg (450,000 volumes), and two institutes at Munich (140,000 and 70,000 volumes). A very large special library (1.1 million volumes) is the library of the World Economics Archives in Hamburg (*Hamburgisches Welt-Wirtschafts-Archiv*), which collects economic and social science literature and is a depository library for many international organizations.

Some special libraries are located abroad. These include the Libraries of the German Archaeological Institute (*Deutsches Archäologisches Institut*) in Athens, Bagdad, Istanbul, Cairo, Lisbon, Madrid, Rome and Teheran, as well as the Library of the Institute of Art History (*Kunsthistorisches Institut*) in Florence (220,000 volumes, 580,000 photos) and the *Bibliotheca Hertziana* in Rome (200,000 volumes), as well as the Libraries of the German Historical Institute (*Deutsches Historisches Institut*) located in London, Paris, Rome, Warsaw and Washington. Their primary areas of collection include archaeology, history, history of art, and oriental studies, and they actively contribute to the scholarly and cultural exchange within the respective host country. Rather modest (11,000 volumes) is the Library of the German Institute for Studies of Japan (*Deutsches Institut für Japanstudien)* in Tokyo.

The *Goethe Institutes* maintain special libraries with literature and media about Germany, and address themselves to a broad public in their host country. They collaborate closely with the language instruction and cultural programs of those Institutes. Since their task is to provide current information, there is a continuous, although slow, turn-over of their holdings; there is no need to archive or keep older materials. The total collection of all *Goethe Institute Libraries* together amounts to approximately 2 million books and other media.

Public Libraries

The public library (*Öffentliche Bibliothek* – ÖB) is the most common type of library in the Federal Republic of Germany: In contrast to the approximately 4,000 academic and research libraries (*Wissenschaftliche Bibliotheken*) there are approximately

A modern city library (*Stadtbibliothek*) was placed in the building of a former slaughterhouse in 1998 in the city of Landau in the Southern Palatinate (Rhineland-Palatinate), in which about 75,000 media units are kept. The materials used in this three-asp construction based on the "house in a house" design were steel, glass, wood, brick, and sandstone.

14,200 public libraries (including school libraries). German cities and communities maintain about 5,400 public libraries and are also responsible for about 4,000 school libraries in their function as the school supporting agency (*Schulträger*). In some Federal states, the counties have established county libraries (*Kreisbibliotheken*) or county and city libraries (*Kreis- und Stadtbibliotheken*), of which about 40 exist. At the level of the parishes and church congregations, the Catholic and the Protes-

The Central Library of the City and State Library (*Stadt- und Landesbibliothek*) in Dortmund (North Rhine-Westphalia) (architect: Mario Botta), newly opened in 1999, sets accents in urban architectural development. In front of a long main building made of stone, there are open access areas in a well-lighted, glass-enclosed area in the form of a dome or rotunda. The collection of the library, which also possesses a large music library, an art library, and a manuscript department, has a total of about 900,000 media units.

tant Churches also sponsor and maintain public libraries (totaling about 5,000).

Community Public Libraries

The community public libraries (*kommunale Bibliotheken*), numbering over 5,400, sometimes call themselves "city libraries" or "community libraries" (*Stadt- bzw. Gemeindebibliotheken*), but generally designate themselves as "city libraries" (*Stadtbibliotheken*). These libraries carry out the basic literature and media provision for the entire population at all levels. They form a tight library network – though in the rural regions there are some "holes." Due to the financial problems of the public support, unfortunately, the number of these libraries is constantly being reduced. Since the operation and maintenance of a public library is based on the voluntary decision of a community to provide suffi-

cient funds for the upkeep of the library, only slightly more than half of the German communities have a community library. Federal subsidies for building and maintaining a city or community library, or for the expansion of the book and media collection, can be obtained in a few Federal states, but in most *Länder*, the financial basis must come completely from the communities.

The public library – independent of how it is supported – makes an important contribution to achieving the basic rights of all citizens laid out in the Constitution and applying to all levels of the population, namely, to "inform oneself from generally accessible resources without hindrances" (Basic Law, Article 5, Paragraph 1). It enables the citizen to participate in the cultural and social life of the community and in doing so, fulfills the requirement that the IFLA expressed 1994 in its *Public Library Manifesto*. With its services and media offerings, the public library fulfills a central service in the educational sector. At the same time, it makes a contribution to realizing of equality of opportunity for each individual person.

In addition to the mission of providing information and general education, public libraries contribute to professional training and continuing education, as well as to the meaningful use of leisure time, and especially to the promotion of reading. In the information society, the transfer of media and information competencies will be increasingly important. Furthermore, the public library has become a place for communication, a meeting point, which has influenced its development towards increasingly becoming a cultural center for events of all kinds.

Public libraries collect non-fiction, part of which also includes scholarly works from all areas of knowledge, professional books for vocational training, reference works of all kinds, journals and newspapers, *belles lettres* and other literature for entertainment, children's and youth books, as well as additional collections which are targeted for special user groups, such as books in languages of the large groups of foreigners living in Germany (Turkish, new Greeks, Russian, etc.). The collection of printed works has been consistently expanded since the 1970's to include new forms of information carriers – first with audiovisual media (videos, language and music cassettes) and games, then later with electronic and digital media (compact discs, CD-ROMs, DVDs) and public access to computer networks, in some instances, also works of art, sheet music, and other music items.

The size of public library collections in the individual Federal *Länder* differs widely and ranges from 2,000 media units in small community libraries run mostly by volunteers up to one to three million media units in individual metropolitan library systems (Berlin, Bremen, Duisburg, Frankfurt/Main, Hamburg, Hanover, Cologne, Lübeck, Munich, etc.). Most libraries in the larger cities (sites with more than 100,000 inhabitants) can offer their users between 150,000 and one million media units. The size recommendation in the "Library Plans" (*Bibliothekspläne*) of 2 media units per inhabitant is only achieved by part of the libraries. In 2001, the funding agencies of public libraries spent an average of 2.35 DM (1.20 Euros) per person in the entire population for purchasing new books and media.

The weekly opening times differ from library to library as well: While most libraries which are completely or partially staffed by volunteers or part-time staff in the communities (frequently found in places with 1,000 to 3,000 inhabitants) are often only open four to eight hours spread out over two days,

Organization of an Expanded
Metropolitan Library System

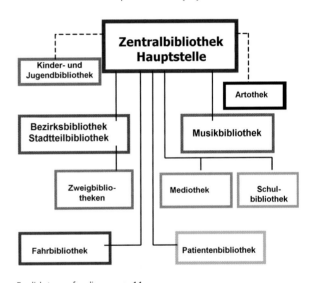

English terms for diagram p. 11

In Germany, about 120 art libraries (*Artotheken* or *Graphotheken*) are supported by either public libraries, community colleges (*Volkshochschulen*) or art associations. These libraries not only lend pictures and other works of art, but also serve to establish contact with contemporary artists and stimulate discussion about modern art. On the average, an *Artothek* holds 1,500 to 2,500 works for loan, primarily reproductions, and also a very limited number of originals. This photo shows the Art Collection of the City and State Library (*Artothek der Stadt- und Landesbibliothek*) of Potsdam (Brandenburg).

libraries in small and middle-sized cities with between 10,000 and 50,000 inhabitants and with
full-time staff provide between 10 and 25 hours of
service which is usually distributed over three to
four days. Most large city libraries are open daily
from Monday to Saturday and reach an average of
more than 40 opening hours per week. With the
exception of many libraries supported by the
churches, community libraries are closed on Sun-
days.

Characteristic for public libraries is to place the
collection in a classified, freely-accessible arrangement. The public library sees itself today as a library
of use (*Gebrauchsbibliothek*) for all patron levels
and thus makes broad and need-oriented book and
non-book collections available. The targeted expansion of offerings oriented to specific user groups,
especially for information purposes, however, has
increased in importance over the last years. Most
libraries orient their acquisitions selection according
to current demand, and weed out titles which are
no longer being used, especially multiple copies.
Only libraries in large cities and the scholarly city
libraries have an archival function for older and

special collections and thus maintain storage
stacks.

The public libraries of larger cities today mostly
join together to form a library system with a central
library and several branch libraries in the suburbs.
In addition to this, there are often special spatially
separate or integrated units, such as children's and
youth libraries, school library, music library, media
center, art collection, and mobile library.

Book busses which take between 3,000 and
6,000 media units on regular rounds are not only
used for communities at the edges of the larger cities, but also in the sparsely populated rural regions.
Approximately 150 mobile libraries are used to substitute for or augment stationary libraries. Their use
is remaining constant at a high level while the number of actual vehicles has gone down. Just as in the
stationary libraries, the mobile libraries are actively
used for promoting reading, hence reading hours
corresponding to the teaching plans at schools and
thematic projects are offered for pre-school groups
and school classes. In the book bus, which stops at
an appointed time in front of the school or the pre-
school, children will have the time to learn, but

Mobile libraries (*Fahrbibliotheken*, also called *mobile
Bibliotheken*, *Autobüchereien* or *Bücherbusse* (book
busses)), are used by about 8% of the counties and
about 5% of the larger cities. These specially converted busses or tractor trucks are now, for the most
part, also equipped with computer installations for
checking out and searching for media. The photos
show the mobile Library of the City Library of
Karlsruhe (*Bücherbus der Stadtbibliothek Karlsruhe*)
(Baden-Württemberg).

The Full Statistics for Public Libraries in 2001: Overview according to Bundesland - inasmuch as statistics were registered

Federal state / Land	Population on 1-1-2001	Population on 1-1-2001 in Library Communities	Number of Libraries Counted	Total Media Units in Collection on 31-12-2001	Number of Circulation Transactions per year	Active Users (lenders)	Visitors (Onsite Users)	Events, Exhibitions, Tours
Baden-Württemberg	10,524,405	9,237,611	1,166	14,805,972	48,165,948	1,240,160	13,434,568	24,254
Bavaria	12,230,255	10,449,556	1,.872	19,963,077	52,397,897	1,557,895	14,260,378	24,530
Berlin	3,382,169	3,382,169	129	4,330,168	12,875,496	63,536	5,109,122	11,279
Brandenburg	2,601,962	1,941,888	328	4,593,580	11,673,046	267,946	2,995,530	7,415
Bremen	660,225	660,225	25	616,829	2,592,810	65,441	1,263,689	2,630
Hamburg	1,715,392	1,715,392	50	1,740,463	9,780,341	146,943	4,500,850	4,535
Hesse	6,068,129	4,628,871	412	4,399,252	10,110,290	320,988	2,576,854	7,413
Mecklenburg-Hinter Pomerania	1,775,703	1,073,037	142	2,858,858	6,523,517	205,383	1,730,369	5,313
Lower Saxony	7,926,193	6,671,847	879	10,048,581	24,537,926	784,925	6,826,669	17,179
North Rhine-Westphalia	18,009,865	17,899,059	2,083	25,686,362	64,268,293	1,993,665	20,704,209	37,674
Rhineland-Palatinate	4,034,557	2,680,676	621	4,233,538	9,124,888	299,249	2,344,425	6,656
Saarland	1,068,703	935,533	121	1,002,549	1,656,737	51,684	531,102	956
Saxony	4,425,581	3,868,064	619	8,211,362	20,325,863	414,725	6,628,909	12,756
Saxony-Anhalt	2,615,375	1,989,630	436	5,257,280	10,117,539	300,280	3,298,991	10,316
Schleswig-Holstein	2,789,761	1,724,023	127	4,182,708	13,285,849	330,865	2,514,516	5,773
Thüringia	2,431,255	1,795,253	317	4,799,714	9,723,122	259,283	3,197,423	6,742
Sum Federal Republic of Germany	82.259.530	70.652.834	9,327	16,730,293	307,159,562	8,302,968	91,917,604	185,421

Source: Deutsche Bibliotheksstatistik (DBS) (German Library Statistics), 2001 – Statistical registration was not complete (EDBI, Berlin) 1) Statistisches Bundesamt Wiesbaden: Population Data from 1 January 2001 – Segment taken from the Basic Community Directory.

above all librarians read to the children, play with them, and do storytelling and art work in order to instill the children and youth with an enthusiasm for working with information and using libraries.

The approximately 3,400 city and community libraries (including branch libraries) which are headed by full-time personnel, stand in contrast to the some 7,000 public libraries headed by volunteers, and of those some 5,000 libraries are funded by the churches and congregations. According to estimates of the associations, almost 25,000 persons are working in small libraries with voluntary staff, while the number of staff positions in the libraries which have full-time directors, approximately 12,500 are employed. Of the approximately 140 million media units in the collections, about 80% are in available in the libraries which are headed by a full-time Librarian. These libraries have approximately 87% of the 340 million cirulation transactions annually. In the year 2001, according to the German Library Statistics approximately 92 million Euros were spent for book and media acquisitions, whereby the percentage in smaller libraries with part-time directors or voluntary staff lies at about 18%.

State Service Centers for Public Libraries

For promoting and advising communal libraries, the German states have established state service centers for public libraries (*Staatliche Fachstellen für Öffentliche Bibliotheken*) on the regional or state level. These are also called *Staatliche Büchereistellen*, *Büchereizentralen* or *Beratungsstellen für Öffentliche Büchereien*. The first of these were founded before and after the First World War (1914–1918), but most of them originated after 1949. Although maintaining community libraries is the task of the municipalities, the states (*Länder*) are nevertheless obliged – because of their responsibility for culture and public education – to build up and develop an effective network of public information.

Today, it is the task of the ca. 32 state service centers for public libraries in the Federal Republic of Germany to support the municipalities in building up libraries which meet professional standards and in developing effective library systems, to advise

The State Service Center for Public Libraries of the Rhineland-Palatinate at Coblence and of the Rhine-Hesse-Palatinate at Neustadt on the Weinstraße jointly issue the periodical *"Die Bücherei – Zeitschrift für Öffentliche Büchereien in Rheinland-Pfalz"* (= The Public Library – Journal for Public Libraries in the Rhineland-Palatinate") since 1952. The cover of the issue depicted here shows a cross-section of the interior of the Andernach City Library (*Stadtbücherei Andernach*) (Rhineland-Palatinate), built in 1990.

state authorities in all issues concerning public libraries, and to give practical help to libraries when needed. The state service centers for public libraries should initiate the founding of new libraries and the expansion of existing libraries, to cooperate in equipping mobile libraries and in the planning of library buildings, to foster the use of new media and technologies, and to support libraries in the fields of public relations, professional staff development, and the promotion of reading and literature. At the same time, they are entrusted with the task of strengthening political and social consciousness for the indispensability of public libraries in modern information society.

Equalizing regional differences, especially breaking down the disparity between urban and rural areas which often causes disadvantages for rural populations in terms of their possibilities of obtaining information and having access to media, is one of the main components in the task of state service centers for public libraries. The services offered by these centers differ from state (*Land*) to state, which, however, makes their work especially beneficial to the public libraries in small and medium-size communities, school libraries, and the institutions which are maintaining these libraries.

As the most important Federal nation-wide authority, the state service centers for public libraries have initiated the "Professional Conference of State Service Centers for Public Libraries in Germany" (*Fachkonferenz der Staatlichen Büchereistellen in Deutschland*), a working committee, in 1962. This collaborative committee sees itself as a forum for supraregional exchange of experience and joint representation of interests. Besides the annual convention, likewise called "*Fachkonferenz*" (Professional Conference), and the coordination of new measures and concepts, the state service center's server, online since 2002, provides access to general professional information about libraries and the topics covered by the state service centers for public libraries through presentation of important documents. In view of the fact that there is no central coordination of public libraries in Germany, these instruments are of national importance.

Public Libraries Supported by Church

Out of 14,895 municipalities in the Federal Republic of Germany, exactly 12,442 had a public library in 1997. Besides 6,118 municipal libraries, there were 4,026 Catholic, 1,045 Protestant, and 1,253 libraries owned by other institutions whereby almost without exception, the ecclesiastical public libraries are located in the old (Western) states. Considering their high number, it must be considered that they lag far behind the municipal libraries concerning holdings, acquisitions budget, and circulation figures, not to speak of opening hours and expenses for personnel. Looking at the literature provision and promotion of reading for children und youth, and at the situation in communities

without a municipal library supported by the community, these church-supported libraries nevertheless play an important role.

Usually, the Catholic or respectively the Protestant parishes maintain the ecclesiastical public libraries. The activities of the Catholic libraries are closely related with that of the *Borromäusverein*, (in Bavaria *St. Michaelsbund*), founded in 1844, and which in Bonn under a different sponsor provides a media and book review service (*Medien- und Lektoratsdienst*) for public libraries. Up until the end of 2003, it operated a state-recognised college for public librarianship and a central library there as well, which however had to be dissolved due to lack of financial support. The central association of Protestant libraries is the German Association of Protestant Public Libraries (*Deutscher Verband evangelischer Büchereien e.V. – DVeB*) in Göttingen. Like the Federal states, the Churches have service centers for their public libraries at the level of the (Catholic) dioceses, respectively (Protestant) regional / state churches (*Landeskirchen*) for support and advisory services for their parish libraries; the 24 Catholic and 14 Protestant library service centers are collaborating in their own joint working committee (*Fachkonferenz*).

A renovated villa combined with an attractive new building made of concrete and glass serves as the home of the City Library of Westerstede (*Stadtbücherei Westerstede*) (Schleswig-Holstein). Approximately 25,000 media units are displayed on 550 sqm of space. The children's library uses motifs of the North Sea coastline with lighthouses and rafts.

Aapproximately 12,000 media units comprise the children's library of the *City Library of Bernburg on the Saale River* (Saxony-Anhalt), completed in the year 2000. This library was furnished with great phantasy and a love of detail which went into the design of an "adventure reading area" (*"Abendteuerlesezone"*). The entire floor covering has the logo of the library worked into it. The total collection numbers some 65,000 media units.

Special Areas of Public Librarianship

Children's and Youth Libraries

Due to the high societal, educational and political significance of library work for children and youth – the key words here are: promoting reading, reading literacy, reading competencies, transmitting literature, bringing youth to literature, media competencies – all public libraries give this target user group their special attention. Children and youth up to the age of 14 use the library much more intensively than any other group of the population and in many cities theyre is a special children's and youth library, or at least a correspondingly equipped department of a public library.

For some time, librarians' special attention has been directed to the age group of four- to twelve-year-olds, and especially for this group, special children's libraries (*Kinderbibliotheken*) or children's departments (*Kinderabteilungen*) were built up, while the literature and media for youth (from 13/14 years) was increasingly integrated into the adult collection. In the children's area, suitable furniture and attractive decorations creates an age-appropriate atmosphere which invites the children to read and to listen, to browse and to play. In addition to books and journals, the visitor finds games, audio-visual media of all kinds, and rapidly increasingly one also finds digital media or an Internet PC for playing games and for informational purposes here. Within the specially scheduled programs of the public libraries, a large portion of time is devoted to activities and events for children and youth.

Many public libraries have a difficult time attracting youth of the age of 14 years-old. Age-appropriate media offerings and events which range from games and Internet PC all the way to musical events or to DVD and CD-circulation are supposed to increasingly attract the youth to the libraries again. Even the offer to participate in the selection of the media or in the decoration of the library rooms are used to awaken a new interest in the library.

School Libraries

The educational and political task of the public library manifests itself particularly well in school libraries where information of all kinds is searched, understood, and processed, but where media competencies and strategies for information use and retrieval can also be transmitted. Despite the well-known significance of school libraries within education – in the year 2000 even more emphasized by the UNESCO manifest "Teaching and Learning with the School Library" – the equipping, furnishing and professional supervision of libraries in many schools of the Federal Republic of Germany is unsatisfactory; inasmuch as the school even has a central collection of books. This lies far below the internationally accepted standards.

The International Youth Library (*Internationale Jugendbibliothek Schloß Blutenburg* – IJB) in Munich (Bavaria), founded in 1948, is a unique research and information center which also offers scholarships and a program of events. The collection comprises about 520,000 books for children and youth, and other media in more than one hundred languages. Several periodicals (*IJB-Report, IJB-Bulletin, The White Ravens*) and directories (*Preisgekrönte Kinderbücher, Die Besten der Besten*) document the worldwide production of books and media for children and youth.

Especially in the primary, middle and junior high schools, school libraries are lacking, but even in the *Gymnasien,* the situation is not very satisfying. Only in a few cases, especially in the newly built *Gymnasien* and comprehensive schools (*Gesamtschulen*), will the standard guidelines and parameters for the use of space, equipment needs for media, and other aspects could be achieved. Although lifelong learning begins in the schools, less than 10% of German schools have adequate library services. The poor results of German pupils in the international comparison of school pupils' achievement (*PISA Studie 2000* of the OECD – Program for International Student Assessment) clearly show the striking negligence of school libraries by those politically responsible for the entire German educational system.

Approximately one third of the school libraries are supplied and taken care of by the local public libraries as publicly accessible branch libraries within a school center. Two thirds of all school libraries, however, exist with independent administration and financing from the school and its community funding agency. Many different forms of practical cooperation between the city library and the school library or media center (*Mediothek*) are possible and are also practiced, as the Bertelsmann Foundation could very impressively prove in its multiyear nation-wide project "Library and School" ("*Bibliothek und Schule*"). In some cities, "school library service centers" (*Schulbibliothekarische Arbeitsstellen*) were established as departments of large city libraries or state service centers for public libraries. With due respect to the rising significance of the Internet, as well as of audiovisual and digital media works used in teaching, the cooperation between the county and the city image archives, as well as with the state media centers (*Landesmedienzentren*) has become more intense. Special programs, which are partially financed by the Federal Government, partially by corporations and businesses or even private persons, serve the purpose of supplying personal computers and Internet access to school libraries.

Library Services to Special User Groups

Library work for special user groups dedicates itself to providing services particular to those persons who are disadvantaged in specific ways or find themselves in difficult life situations. Included in this group, are first of all, physically disabled or blind persons, but also patients in hospitals and prison inmates.

To provide the ca. 140,000 blind in Germany with information and literature, there are a dozen libraries for the blind (*Blindenbibliotheken*), mostly organized by associations under civil law. Their total holdings comprise ca. 200,000 audio-books (audio-cassette or compact disc) and 150,000 books, periodicals and music books in the raised dot letters developed by Louis Braille. The prevailing form of lending is via the postal service. The offerings of the libraries for the blind are complemented by those of the ecclesiastical institutions, departments for the blind in some metropolitan libraries, digital writing-to-speech-converters (e.g. in *Die Deutsche Bibliothek*), and other facilities.

About eight percent of the roughly 5,000 German hospitals funded by public, ecclesiastical or private funding agencies have patient libraries (*Patientenbibliotheken*), offering patients and hospital personnel literature and other media. The holdings, averaging 6,000 to 8,000 media units, should be part of a holistic concept of health care to promote recovery of the patients and to cover their desire for information concerning illnesses. To be distinguished from those patient libraries, there are also special medical libraries (*medizinische Fachbibliotheken*) available for use by the clinic's physicians which have to be considered as scientific special libraries.

Small prison libraries (*Gefängnisbibliotheken*), on the average holding about 2,500 media units, exist in prisons, which in Germany are under the responsibility of the Federal states (*Länder*). The provision of literature in hospitals and prisons (= social library work – *Soziale Bibliotheksarbeit*) are among those fields of library work which are particularly affected by financial cuts of public and ecclesiastical organizations. However, in contrast to the reasons for reduction, precisely these libraries urgently need social and political upgrading and the respective financial support.

Other Libraries

Besides those already mentioned, there are other libraries, comparable in their function to public libraries, but open to a limited group of users only. For instance, the German Military Forces (*Deutsche Bundeswehr*) maintain numerous smaller "troop libraries" (*Truppenbüchereien*) in addition to its military special libraries, which provide general information and entertainment for the soldiers, and for this purpose also offer in particular audio-media as well. Only members of companies have access to the company libraries – still numbering about 100 company libraries (*Werkbibliotheken*) – essentially smaller public libraries for the workers of that particular company. These *Werkbibliotheken* serve to provide information, professional training and continuing education, general further education and leisure time activities, and with that clearly distinguish themselves from the company technical libraries or corporate libraries, which serve research and development and belong to that particular type of special library (corporate libraries).

Documentation Centers

With the "Program of the Federal Government for Enhancing Information and Documentation, 1974 – 1977" (*Programm der Bundesregierung zur Förderung von Information and Dokumentation 1974 – 1977 – also referred to as the IuD-Program*), the systematic development of a network of information- and documentation centers began. Since subject-oriented information is fundamentally seen as a commercial enterprise branch which has to earn its place on the market, the first of these IuD-position papers saw itself – and those following even more clearly – as a contribution to the advancement of the economy rather than of science. Hence, from the very beginning, the main emphasis of these position papers (or programs) was placed more on the field of the sciences and engineering.

The most important outcome of the IuD-Programs which affected libraries, was the formation of subject-oriented information systems (*Fachinformationssysteme* – FIS) with subject-oriented information centers (*Fachinformationszentren* – FIZ) by combining already existing institutions. The development of subject-specific databases and increased databases of relevant titles in scientific literature, led to a rising demand for such documents, especially for journal articles. From the very beginning, it was the task of the Central Subject Libraries (*Zentrale Fachbibliotheken*) to provide the documents indexed in the databases of the subject information centers (*Fachinformationszentren*) whereas today it is accomplished in part by the *Fachinformationszentren* themselves using electronic delivery. Since *Fachinformation* is a commercial commodity, there is a charge for all services from searching to document delivery.

The *Fachinformationszentrum Karlsruhe GmbH* (often called *FIZ Karlsruhe*), a non-profit service institution, is an example of a renowned institute charged with the task of providing highly specialized, high quality information for research in science and industry and making it available in a form which can be processed easily and rapidly. Since 1983, *FIZ Karlsruhe* hosts *STN International* (*Scientific and Technical Information Network*) for all of Europe as its main function. *STN International* is one of the leading online services for scientific and technical databases: 210 bibliographic and factual databases with ca. 350 million structured documents can be reached via the online networks. All branches of the natural sciences and technology, as well as international patent information are included. In cooperation with partner libraries, among them the German Central Subject Libraries (*Zentrale Fachbibliotheken*), *FIZ Karlsruhe* provides the necessary primary sources for its clients.

Besides *FIZ Karlsruhe* and DIMDI (previously mentioned) at Cologne, there are some further subject information centers (*Fachinformationszentren*) and documentation institutions (*Dokumentationseinrichtungen*), including ones for technology (Frankfurt/Main), chemistry (Berlin), construction and space (Stuttgart), agriculture (Bonn), law, and psychology (both at Saarbrücken).

Since 1999, the policies regarding subject information centers of the Federal Republic of Germany have come under the influence of the "Digital Library." The strategic position paper "Networking Information – Activating Knowledge" (*Information vernetzen – Wissen aktivieren*), published in 2002, recognizes the Federal Government's obligation "to ensure access to published information and to ensure provision of scientific information to [those working in] education and research, to preserve the knowledge acquired thusfar with the understanding of maintaining cultural diversity, to avoid the digital divide within society, and to strengthen the competencies of all citizens to be able to deal with information efficiently and critically."

4 PROFESSIONS AND ASSOCIATIONS

The Organization(s) of German Librarianship

The Librarian Professions

Librarians are professionals for the transfer of all types of stored information and for dealing with the important raw material "knowledge" – totally independent of whether they are employed in a university library, a school library, or in the special business library (corporate library). Their tasks of collecting, managing, indexing and cataloging, and acting as intermediary for books and other media makes them professional partners in the media and information fields. Already today, and definitely much more intensely in the future, they are navigators in the data networks; they make electronic information accessible and ensure its quality and relevance.

In Germany, the spectrum of library work has expanded considerably with the changing demands on libraries and this is not just due to the rapid development of information and communications technology. The expectations which library users today place on the use of and knowledge transfer via media, information and reference services differ quite decisively from the queries and information needs of users twenty or thirty years ago. These expectation levels most certainly result from the growing democratic self-consciousness of the citizens who demand – and rightfully so – that the modern library be a more user-friendly, competent, timely, and well-equipped service unit.

The professions in the areas of information, literature, and modern media have gained new meaning and breadth during the last decades. In addition to the professions "librarian" (*Bibliothekar*), "documentalist" or "information specialist" (*Dokumentar*), "archivist" (*Archivar*), trained technical staff for media and information services (*Fachangestellter für Medien- und Informationsdienste*), as well as *Information Brokers,* have evolved – all of which are branches of the information profession with their areas of activity moving closer together despite remaining distinctions: While *information brokers* deal more with the "marketable aspects" of information and acquire these via data networks

for commercial purposes, *documentalists* in documentation and information centers ensure there is an optimal indexing structure and that there is current information on data from economics, research, and technology. A*rchivists* in most of the community and state archives are concerned with the storage and indexing of documents and other resources from the past and the present. The *trained technical staff* in libraries, information centers, and data centers are now being employed in all these professions in the function of a technical assistant. Among these four professional groups, librarians (*Bibliothekare*) and more recently the information managers (*Informationswirte*) in the various types of libraries form an indispensable connection with their media collections and palette of service offerings.

Today there are approximately 18,000 full-time trained professionals in Germany in the broad area of libraries and similar institutions. In addition, there are 25,000 volunteers or part-time staff in smaller public libraries and school libraries supported by municipalities and churches, and who acquire their practical skills for their library and information work through continuing education courses and training sessions.

Within the professions of librarian or information manager, documentalist, and archivist, an even stronger – though parallel – division of tasks has taken place which has virtually developed into a speciality of its own. This transition is much more apparent in Germany than in the more pragmatically oriented Anglo-Saxon countries. Partially responsible for this splitting of the three professions into various professional associations and groups is probably the geographical and intellectual historically determined desire for decentralization (perhaps even delimitation) – a fundamental principle which has certainly evoked many positive developments in German federalism, but in several areas has also produced more of a "particularism" with all its negative consequences.

The rapid development of information and communications technologies and the transition to the information and service society has not only changed the professional landscape of librarians extensively here in Germany; in these expanding areas of work, many see significant chances for growth and development, while in other branches, the labor market is tending towards stagnation. This transition goes hand in hand with the noticeable convergence of related or "neighboring" professions, or professions originally categorized elsewhere. Thus, new areas of employment have evolved, such as electronic publishing, multimedia, cultural industry, and media design.

The noticeable convergence in professional training for the different information professions has been preceded by a long period – influenced by tradition in Germany – of delimitation and distinct separation: the formation of the professional image has been influenced over the decades by the separation of the various divisions (*Spartentrennung*) between public librarianship on the one hand, and academic and research librarianship on the other, as well as between the librarian and documentalist activities. Even within library personnel, one finds a segmented and even more subdivided professional landscape.

If one asks about the reasons for this separation, then the background of this development is less likely to be found in the structure of German libra-

rianship. Instead, it is primarily the result of the German labor and professional occupational laws. Since the end of the 19th century, civil service careers for the so-called scientific (academic and research) library service (*Beamtenlaufbahnen für den sog. wissenschaftlichen Bibliotheksdienst*) were established, and with them certain hierarchies and corresponding regulations which led to the prominent, pronounced status consciousness and within it the associated need for separating themselves from others. Client-oriented or service-oriented characteristics were not taken into consideration.

At the beginning of the 21st century, the distinction between the professional sectors is fading more and more, and the sections are opening themselves favorably to a differentiation of libraries and their staff according to size, targeted user groups, the level of qualifications, or even according to the performance level of the libraries and the comprehensiveness of their services. Within the professions and their required training, the main emphasis in the future will be on the basic core of commonly needed key qualifications, skills, and competencies across the professions which will be demanded of any person working in a library.

In libraries financed by public funds, library staff are either employed as salaried employees or as civil servants.[1] Library staff given the rank of civil servant are obligated to their employer in a service and loyalty relationship, and they are paid according to Federal or state laws. Library staff in an "employee" relationship (*Angestellte*) are paid accord-

---

[1] The status of these two groups may not be clear from the names of these positions as in some countries these terms have no apparent difference in meaning: however, in Germany, the employee (*Angestellter*) does not qualify for certain amenities that the civil servant (*Beamte*) will have (higher pension, etc.). A foreigner can be an employee, but German citizenship is necessary to be a civil servant. Furthermore, civil service positions cannot be cancelled during downsizing, although employee positions can. (*Translator's note*)

One of main tasks of the librarian is to serve as a navigator in an increasingly complex media jungle and to filter the specific data out of the flood of information which the library user needs for his or her concrete purposes. This photograph shows a poster to this end with which the City Library of Essen (North Rhine-Westphalia) advertises – even in the Internet.

ing to private law and are subject to the collective wage agreements called "The Federal Employees' Wage Rates" (*Bundesangestelltentarif – BAT*), which are negotiated by the unions and the public employers.

In the entire area of public service, *Beamte* and the corresponding *Angestelle* are arranged into different career level groups depending on the level of education and training: the unskilled (*einfachen*), the skilled or "middle" (*mittleren*), the upper (*gehobenen*), and the senior (*höheren*) service levels. The salary or pay scale of library personnel is also regulated according to these groups. The assignment to a certain group or level depends on the person's prior education and training, as well as on the job description. A similar arrangement applies for the staff of libraries which have churches as employers. However, the situation is different for library personnel in any kind of corporation; in these businesses, the employment contract is usually be negotiated individually and is subject to civil law; salaries are often similar to the wage scales negotiated by the trade unions and public service employers or only slightly higher.

The History of Professional Librarian Training

The education and training for librarianship and all similar professions have been in constant transition during the last two decades. To try to give a conclusive, exact portrayal of the entire situation would be presumptuous. The continuing change expresses on the one hand the political desire to adapt to the current developments and to the modernization of the content of librarian education, but also demonstrates on the other hand the uncertainties of the political decision-makers who, motivated by the necessity to reduce costs, see the amalgamation and fusion of institutions as the universal remedy.

Formal training for the librarian profession in Germany only began at the end of the 19th century. In 1893, the Prussian government decreed an ordinance which prescribed professional training, and determined the content of this training. Persons who had completed a university degree and who aspired to the profession of librarian would also have to successfully complete a postgraduate training program. The training program for the subject specialist in civil service (*Referendarausbildung*) can

Professions in Public and Academic/Research Libraries (Public Service)
Overview of Career Levels

Funktionsbezeichnung Angestellte	Amtsbezeichnung Beamte	Vergütungs-/ Besoldungs-gruppe
Leiter der Stadtbibliothek Amtsleiter Stadtbibliothek	Leitender Bibliotheksdirektor	Verg.-Gr. BAT I, Bes.-Gr. A 16
Leiter der Stadtbibliothek Amtsleiter Stadtbibliothek	Bibliotheksdirektor	Verg.-Gr. BAT Ia, Bes.-Gr. A 15
Leiter der Stadtbibliothek Stellv. Bibliotheksleiter	Oberbibliotheksrat	Verg.-Gr. BAT Ib, Bes.-Gr. A 14
Leiter der Stadtbibliothek Stellv. Bibliotheksleiter Abteilungsleiter	Bibliotheksrat (h.D.) Oberamtsrat (g.D.)	Verg.-Gr. BAT IIa, Bes.-Gr. A 13
Leiter der Stadtbibliothek Stellv. Bibliotheksleiter Abteilungsleiter	Bibliotheksamtsrat	Verg.-Gr. BAT III, Bes.-Gr. A 12
Leiter der Stadtbibliothek Stellv. Bibliotheksleiter Abteilungsleiter	Bibliotheksamtmann	Verg.-Gr. BAT IVa, Bes.-Gr. A 11
Leiter der Stadtbibliothek Stellv. Bibliotheksleiter Zweigstellenleiter	Bibliotheksoberinspektor	Verg.-Gr. BAT IVb, Bes.-Gr. A 10
Leiter der Stadtbibliothek Stellv. Bibliotheksleiter Zweigstellenleiter	Bibliotheksinspektor (g.D.) Amtsinspektor (m.D.)	Verg.-Gr. BAT Vb, Bes.-Gr. A 9
Assistent an Bibliotheken Fachangestellter	Bibliothekshauptsekretär	Verg.-Gr. BAT Vc, Bes.-Gr. A 8
Assistent an Bibliotheken Fachangestellter	Bibliotheksobersekretär	Verg.-Gr. BAT VIb, Bes.-Gr. A 7
Assistent an Bibliotheken Fachangestellter	Bibliothekssekretär	Verg.-Gr. BAT VIII/VII, Bes.-Gr. A 6/A5

Explanation:
Blue outline: Senior Service
Red outline: Upper Service
Brown outline: Skilled (Middle) Service

English terms for diagram p. 11

thus be traced back to this Prussian regulation, as well as to the ordinance of the Bavarian government in 1905, which for decades has been the standard method of training for academic and research librarians. In some states (*Länder*), this method of training still exists in this same manner today. The professional librarian training, upon which most of the courses of study in the universities for applied science (for the certified librarian) are based, began in 1914 with the founding of the first library school in Leipzig.

· The course of study for the certified librarian (*Diplom-Bibliothekar*) or for the certified information manager (*Diplom-Informationswirt*) – as the newest professional designation is called – is generally located at the level of the university of applied science today. The previous "library schools" first became independent universities of applied science with only library, documentalist, and archival training programs; in the meantime, they have become departments of larger universities of applied sciences with corresponding courses of study. The length of study lies between seven and eight semesters; within these are several practica of differing duration or even practical semesters. As opposed to the university courses of study, practical experience plays an important role here. In Federal civil service, state civil service, and civil service in the municipalities, library staff with this qualification belong to the level of the upper civil service (*gehobener Dienst*). At the level of senior service (*höherer Dienst*), most often librarians with a previously completed university degree are employed and given duties which require the ability to do research work. Usually, these persons have completed a special additional post-graduate librarian training program after their first degree of university studies. This additional qualification takes place either in the form of four semesters of graduate study or a two-year training program, in some cases as candidate for the higher civil service (status as *Beamte*) and in some cases as a free course of

study (status as "student"). The additional course of study or training program is divided into theory and practice: the practical part takes place in an academic and research library certified as a training library; the theoretical part takes place at an institution of higher education (university). The training program ends with the completion of the state civil service examination for the higher civil service (state examination – *Staatsexamen*). The graduate degree program is completed with the qualification "scientific librarian" (*Wissenschaftlicher Bibliothekar*), "Magister Artium" (M.A.) or "Master of Library and Information Science" (MLIS).

Typical areas of responsibility in the senior civil service position in academic and research libraries are literature selection and classification of subject literature, reference and advisory services, coordination of internal and external library organization, and planning of and cooperation in projects involving new information technologies.

In reality in larger libraries, the professions are divided into four levels according to the hierarchy of tasks: the academic and research librarians with a completed subject study at the university level (level 1), the certified librarians / certified information managers with a degree from a university of

Division of Library Professions with Selected Activities Using the Example of a Metropolitan Library

Beispiele für Tätigkeiten im Vergleich

Universitätsstudium

Höherer Dienst

1. **Bestands- und Informationsvermittlung:**
Auskünfte und Beratung bei wissenschaftlichen Fragestellungen
2. **Werbung und Öffentlichkeitsarbeit:**
wissenschaftliche Ausstellungen, Planung und Koordination des Kulturmanagements insgesamt
3. **Bestandsaufbau und Erwerbung**
Erstellen eines Bestandskonzepts, Inhaltliche Verantwortung für Beanstandsaufbau, Lektorat, Verantwortung für Erwerbungsetat

FH-Studium

Gehobener Dienst

1. **Bestands- und Informationsvermittlung:**
Recherchen in Nachschlagewerken, Datenbanken, Datennetzen
2. **Werbung und Öffentlichkeitsarbeit:**
Fachvorträge halten, Organisation bibliographischer Dienste
3. **Bestandsaufbau und Erwerbung:**
Koordinierung des Bestandsaufbaus, Aushandeln von Lieferkonditionen und Vereinbarungen

Berufsausbildung

Mittlerer Dienst

1. **Bestands- und Informationsvermittlung:**
Erarbeitung von Dokumentationen, Auskünfte bei Standortfragen
2. **Werbung und Öffentlichkeitsarbeit:**
Mitarbeiterschulungen und Klassenführungen durchführen
3. **Bestandsaufbau und Erwerbung:**
Durchführen der Inventarisierung, Rechnungsbearbeitung
Führen der Haushaltsüberwachungslisten

Anlerntätigkeit

Einfacher Dienst

1. **Bestands- und Informationsvermittlung:**
Technische Abwicklung des Leihverkehrs, Versand von Fotokopien
2. **Werbung und Öffentlichkeitsarbeit:**
Werbeblätter drucken, kopieren und versenden
3 **Bestandsaufbau und Erwerbung**:
Anlegen von Statistiken, Annahme von Lieferungen, Schreiben und Übermitteln von Bestellungen, Botengänge

English terms for diagram p. 11

65

State of the art working areas in libraries of institutions of higher education support students and accompany their training and study with book and non-book materials. This photograph shows the Multimedia Reading Room of *Die Deutsche Bibliothek* in Frankfurt/Main (Hesse), equipped with modern technology and a system for multimedia provision which assists in the registration, administration, search and retrieval, and presentation of electronic publications.

applied science (level 2), the so-called professional skilled employee for media and information service (*Fachangestellte für Medien- und Informationsdienste*) or library assistants (*Bibliotheksassistenten*) (level 3), as well as the semi-skilled library employee (*Bibliotheksangestellte*) (level 4).

· The professional skilled employees for media and information service ("*Fachangestellte für Medien- und Informationsdienste*") are trained, as portrayed above, within the framework of the dual system vocational training for the duration of three years in information and documentation centers for all tasks ascribed to library and information assistants; in public civil service, they are located at the middle level ("*mittlerer Dienst*").

A special aspect of this training program, established in 1999, is that its content is oriented to five different specialties of study: in addition to libraries, the semi-skilled trainees can concentrate their training on archives, general information and documentation centers, photo agencies, and medical documentation units. Vocational education committees in the chambers of commerce (*Industrie- und Handelskammer* – IHK) and other responsible jurisdiction units of the district governments of the individual *Länder* exercise advisory and coordination functions for this training. A Federal framework plan and a program for the on-the-job training define the sequence, the goals, and the content of the dual school- and job-oriented training program. The requirement for admission to the professional training program is usually successful completion of the 10th grade (in German the *Mittlere Reife* equivalent to the General Certificate of Education, Ordinary Level in Great Britain).

Librarian Training and Institutions for Library Training in Germany

Courses of study for the librarian professions at universities, institutions of higher education and universities of applied science are possible today at a total of 11 places in Germany. These training institutions can be categorized as follows:

· Library Schools (*Bibliotheksschulen*) in which training Is offered for the skilled (middle – *mittlerer*) or senior (*höherer*) service in libraries, or for the profession of semi-skilled library employee with the specialisation "library"; or

· Departments for Library and Information Science (*Fachbereiche für Bibliotheks- und Informationswesen*) at public polytechnics or administrative academies which often train for employment in internal administration; or

· Universities of Applied Science for Librarianship and Information Services (*Fachhochschulen für Bibliotheks- und Informationswesen*) at which the course of study for the certified librarian (*Diplom-Bibliothekar*) is offered; or

· University Degree Programs in Library Science (*universitäre Studiengänge der Bibliothekswissenschaft*). Only one of such degree program currently exists at the Humboldt University in Berlin at the *Institute for Library Science* (*Institut für Bibliothekswissenschaft*), as well as in a cooperative course of study between the Humboldt University and the University of Coblenz-Landau in a special distance education program as a minor subject of study for the Coblence and Landau students.

Librarian Training Institutions in Germany

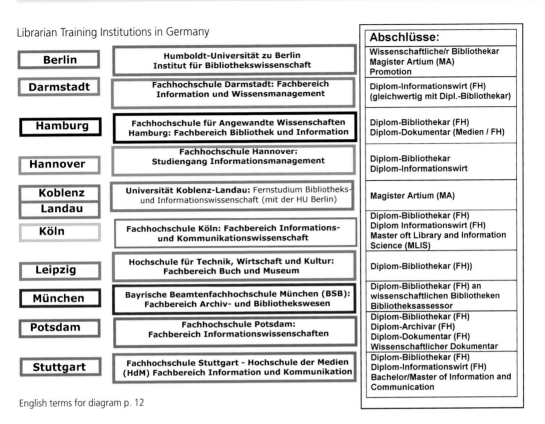

		Abschlüsse:
Berlin	Humboldt-Universität zu Berlin Institut für Bibliothekswissenschaft	Wissenschaftliche/r Bibliothekar Magister Artium (MA) Promotion
Darmstadt	Fachhochschule Darmstadt: Fachbereich Information und Wissensmanagement	Diplom-Informationswirt (FH) (gleichwertig mit Dipl.-Bibliothekar)
Hamburg	Fachhochschule für Angewandte Wissenschaften Hamburg: Fachbereich Bibliothek und Information	Diplom-Bibliothekar (FH) Diplom-Dokumentar (Medien / FH)
Hannover	Fachhochschule Hannover: Studiengang Informationsmanagement	Diplom-Bibliothekar Diplom-Informationswirt
Koblenz Landau	Universität Koblenz-Landau: Fernstudium Bibliotheks- und Informationswissenschaft (mit der HU Berlin)	Magister Artium (MA)
Köln	Fachhochschule Köln: Fachbereich Informations- und Kommunikationswissenschaft	Diplom-Bibliothekar (FH) Diplom Informationswirt (FH) Master oft Library and Information Science (MLIS)
Leipzig	Hochschule für Technik, Wirtschaft und Kultur: Fachbereich Buch und Museum	Diplom-Bibliothekar (FH))
München	Bayrische Beamtenfachhochschule München (BSB): Fachbereich Archiv- und Bibliothekswesen	Diplom-Bibliothekar (FH) an wissenschaftlichen Bibliotheken Bibliotheksassessor
Potsdam	Fachhochschule Potsdam: Fachbereich Informationswissenschaften	Diplom-Bibliothekar (FH) Diplom-Archivar (FH) Diplom-Dokumentar (FH) Wissenschaftlicher Dokumentar
Stuttgart	Fachhochschule Stuttgart - Hochschule der Medien (HdM) Fachbereich Information und Kommunikation	Diplom-Bibliothekar (FH) Diplom-Informationswirt (FH) Bachelor/Master of Information and Communication

English terms for diagram p. 12

Continuing Professional Education and Further Education for Library Staff [2]

In order to do proper justice to the rising professional requirements, a systematic and well-structured program of continuing professional education and further education of library personnel in the sense of life-long learning is necessary. Continuing professional education includes here, above all, the organization of activities leading to qualifications in context of internal staff development as an important component of library management.

In Germany, there are many suppliers of continuing professional education for librarians; foremost among them are:
· the professional associations and their regional chapters
· the union catalogs, the State libraries, university libraries, and regional libraries (Landesbibliotheken)
· the institutions of higher education which have librarian training programs
· state service centers for public libraries and church library service centers
· larger city libraries
· the ministries and administrative authorities
· the chambers of commerce (for gaining the qualification of trainer)
· the ekz-Library Service, Inc. (ekz-Bibliotheksservice GmbH)
· commercial enterprises and foundations, private institutions, societies and associations in the educational and cultural sectors.

Approximate 1,000 continuing professional education events for librarians are offered annually which are very comprehensive and varied, although a uni-

---

[2] Germans distinguish between "continuing professional education" which is in the professional field one has had training in and "further education" which is not necessarily in the field in which one has had training. (Translator's note)

fied coordination of the continuing education suppliers is still lacking in Germany. Since the dissolution of the German Library Institute, the rebuilding of a coordinating unit with a nation-wide database of continuing education events for librarians remains an important desiderata.

In order to meet the national and international standards for a practical, professionally-oriented program of further education, which could also open new opportunities for professional development for the graduates of the librarian training institutions, the Federation of German Library Associations (*Bundesvereinigung Deutscher Bibliotheksverbände – BDB*) founded the so-called "Certification Board" (*Zertifizierungsboard*) in the year 2002, and commissioned a group of experts to develop a generally recognized concept for continuing education. Under the motto *"IQ 2000"* (*Initiative Qualifizierung* = Initiative for Qualification), several certified professional continuing education events have been made available since the beginning of 2002 through the union catalog centers and libraries of institutions of higher education. For example, online searching courses for library staff are offered by the reference and advisory service of the Higher Education Library Center (*Hochschulbibliothekszentrum – HBZ*) in Cologne, or certification courses in "Library Management" are offered at the Free University of Berlin.

Institutional Cooperation Among Libraries in Germany

The large variety of independent libraries with various financiers is a result of the cultural autonomy and the federated structure of the Federal Republic of Germany. This variety provides extensive opportunities for individual development and creative methods. However, this individualization also inherently breeds the danger of fragmentation. Since, however, no library can fulfill its tasks completely by itself, cooperation between libraries and the creation of institutions with central functions and services are of major significance. In this sense, the goal is not only to save libraries from unnecessary duplicated work and to improve the libraries' services; rather, the intention to work against fragmentation by means of suitable strategic and structural measures of library policy and politics is the foremost goal.

Since the beginning of the 20th century, various library organizations, institutions, and associations with supraregional (national) significance have been created which have moulded librarianship in Germany and repeatedly provided it with new impulses for further development. In part, they can look back on a long tradition.

The fact that library cooperation has not been directed or organized by state authorities has produced various advantages and disadvantages. This cooperation takes place primarily in societies and associations which are organized on the basis of German civil law. In this respect, one must differentiate between professional societies of librarians as persons (*Personalvereine*) and institutional associations (*Institutionenverbände*). Societies of librarians (*Personalvereine*) are organizations in which librarians and other library personnel have banded together to protect their professional interests. At the same time, they serve as forums for professional discussion and a means of joint representation in public. The institutional associations (*Institutionenverbände*) are combinations of libraries, library institutions, and supporting institutions of libraries which pursue the common goal of promoting recognition of library duties, developing unified standards, and strengthening the political position of the library (and librarians) in politics and society.

The attempted fusion in the middle of the 1990's of the previous four (today two) librarian associations, BIB and VDB, with the institutional association DBV to one unified association in Germany did not succeed. The task of building an association structure, as has been demonstrated in Switzerland, Great Britain, the United States, or on the international level in the IFLA, remains one of the long-term goals of the association work for many library professionals in Germany.

The most important organizations are those societies and associations, institutions and foundations joined together today under the "umbrella" of the Federation of German Library Associations (*Bundesvereinigung Deutscher Bibliotheksverbände e.V – BDB*). In addition to the association-based organizations, most recently foundations and privately organized institutions, foremostly the *Bertelsmann Foundation* and the *Goethe Institute Inter Nationes*, have increasingly participated as patrons of librarianship and as active members of the BDB.

Bundesvereinigung
Deutscher
Bibliotheksverbände

Members of the Federation of German
Library Associations

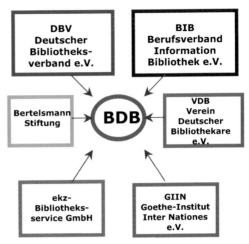

English terms for diagram p. 12

The Bundesvereinigung Deutscher Bibliotheksverbände e.V. (BDB) as Federation of German Library Associations

The standardized professional and political requirements for intensifying the cooperation among libraries and their representation in public were established for the first time in Germany in the 1960's and 1970's with the creation of the German Library Conference (*Deutschen Bibliothekskonferenz – DBK*), founded in 1963, and the compilation of the *Bibliotheksplan '73*. To focus even more on the portrayal of the library and its image in public, the *Bundesvereinigung Deutscher Bibliotheksverbände e.V.* (BDB) was founded in September 1989 as the successor of the German Library Conference.

The BDB as umbrella organization for all library associations, with its headquarters in Berlin, is a chartered association (*eingetragener Verein, e.V.*) with its own constitution. The association's organizational bodies are the general assembly, the executive board, and the speaker as the head of the board, who represents German librarianship externally during a three-year term of office. Since 1999, the board can institute temporary task forces and continuing commissions.

An important aspect of the platform of the BDB is the foreign work and representation of German librarianship which is supported by contributions from the German Foreign Office (*Auswärtiges Amt*) in Berlin and the cultural foundation of the *Länder*. The foundation "Library & Information International" (*Bibliothek & Information International – BII*), which is currently located in the State and University Library of Hamburg (*Staats- und Universitätsbibliothek Hamburg*), is working towards an intensification of international contacts in conjunction with the *Goethe-Institute Inter Nationes*, the *Bertelsmann Stiftung,* and the German Society for Information Science and Information Practice

(*Deutsche Gesellschaft für Informationswissenschaft und Informationspraxis – DGI*). The BII promotes the exchange of experience and information through study trips and periods of foreign work for foreign and German librarians. The BDB is a member of the *European Bureau of Library, Information and Documentation Associations (EBLIDA).*

The regular exchange between representatives of municipal libraries and state service centers for public libraries with the central associations, such as the Standing Conference of Cultural Ministers (KMK), has been established in the "Platform of Public Libraries" (*Plattform Öffentliche Bibliotheken*) of the BDB.

Since 1996, the BDB, together with the German Literature Conference, awards the "Karl Preusker Medal" (*Karl-Preusker-Medaille*) in memory of the founder of the first public library of Germany in Großenhain. The award goes to a person whose commitment and special service to public librarianship deserves high recognition.

The publication of the BDB is the monthly journal *Bibliotheksdienst*. The BDB sponsors the German Library Congress (*Deutscher Bibliothekskongress*) at three-year intervals as the largest professional conference in Germany. Leipzig (1993 and 2000) and Dortmund (1994 and 1997) were previous Congress venues; as of 2004, this professional Congress will take place every three years in the city of Leipzig.

Deutscher Bibliotheksverband e.V. (DBV)

The history of the German Libraries Association (*Deutscher Bibliotheksverband* – DBV) began in 1949 in the Western part of divided Germany. In the GDR, a separate German Libraries Association (*Deutscher Bibliotheksverband* – DBV) emerged, which as a professional body, united the libraries with full-time directors, as well as professional institutions and those for information and documentation, and until 1990 was called the Library Association of the German Democratic Republic (*Bibliotheksverband der Deutschen Demokratischen Republik*).

After reunification of Germany, the West German and the East German Library Associations converged to become the current German Library Association (*Deutscher Bibliotheksverband e.V. – DBV*). This new, cross-sectional institutional association now has approximately 2,000 members. Regular membership is open to all libraries with a full-time director, state and church library service centers, as well as other institutions of librarianship and documentation.

The DBV has defined its mission to promote German librarianship and cooperation among libraries and librarian institutions by formulating political demands for improving librarianship and by taking an official stand on fundamental professional issues by means of professional certificates and recommendations. Important parts of its spectrum of activities are:

· Developing unified, effective solutions to librarians' professional issues and helping to strategically place these within the profession,
· Public portrayal of the objectives and functions of libraries, but also of their deficits and problem areas,
· Lobbying, negotiating, and maintaining contacts with members of Parliament and the ministries at the Federal and *Länder* level, with municipalities, municipal central authorities, and regional corporate bodies,
· Initiating and accompanying professional surveys in cooperation with central library institutions

Deutscher
Bibliotheksverband e.V.

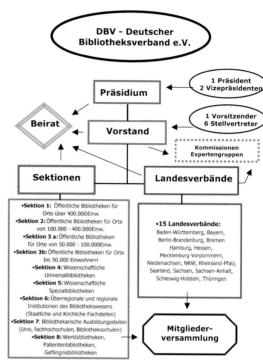

The Association Bodies and Division of the DBV in Sections and Regional Branches (*Landesverbände*)
English terms for diagram p. 12

· Developing promotional activities together with the German Research Council (*Deutsche Forschungsgemeinschaft*) and with the Federal and State Commission for Library Planning and Advancement of Research (*Bund-Länder-Kommission für Bildungsplanung und Forschungsförderung – BLK*),
· Organizing and carrying out professional information events and continuing professional education offerings,
· Improving European and international cooperation in librarianship and integrating foreign experiences into German library practice.

Examples of subject-specific professional publication activities of the DBV include:
· *Die Öffentliche Bibliothek – Standortbestimmung und Zukunftsperspektiven* (1989) ("The Public Library – Determination of its position and future perspectives")
· *Die Wissenschaftliche Bibliothek – Aufgaben, Wandlungen, Probleme* (1993) ("The Academic and Research Library: Its Tasks, Transitions, Problems")

· *Zur Frage der Benutzungsgebühren in Öffent-lichen Bibliotheken* (1994) ("On the Question of User Fees in Public Libraries")
· *Bibliotheken im Zeitalter der Datenautobahnen und internationalen Netze* (1995) ("Libraries in the Age of Data Highways and International Networks")
· *Ehrenamtliche Arbeit in Bibliotheken* (1996 und 1999) ("Volunteer Work in Libraries").

Two divisions of the DBV deserve special mention here:

The Association of Libraries of the State of North Rhine-Westphalia (*Verband der Bibliotheken des Landes Nordrhein-Westfalen e.V* – VBNW), founded in 1948, represents both academic and research libraries and public libraries and was accepted in the DBV in the function of a State library association ("*Landesverband*"). It has approximately 330 members and publishes its own, nationally regarded professional journal, *Pro Libris*.

The German Special Libraries Association (*Arbeitsgemeinschaft der Spezialbibliotheken e.V.* – ASpB), founded in 1946, is a member of Section 5 of the DBV and allows both institutional and personal memberships. Currently, it has 676 members. Its intention is to promote cooperation between special libraries, represent the interests of this particular type of library in the public sphere, and to contribute to exchange of professional experience and deepening of professional knowledge. To this end, the ASpB hosts professional conferences every two years; the results of these conferences are published regularly.

Instigated by the DBV, the German Initiative for Networked Information (*Deutsche Initiative für Netzwerkinformation e.V.* – DINI) founded in 2000, includes the Centers for Communication and Information Processing in Teaching and Research (*Zentren für Kommunikation und Informationsverarbeitung in Lehre und Forschung – ZKI*), the Association of Media Centers at German Institutions of Higher Education (*Arbeitsgemeinschaft der Me-*

dienzentren der deutschen Hochschulen – AMH), and the Information and Communication Commission of the German Learned Societies (*IuK-Initiative der deutschen Fachgesellschaften*) as cooperative partners. The goal of this innovative association, which is supported with project funding from the German Research Council (DFG), is to improve information and communication services and to promote the necessary infrastructure development in higher education and in the learned societies at a regional and national level by promoting corresponding standards, recommendations, and projects.

To promote libraries and to ensure their educational effectiveness, the DBV founded the Helmut Sontag Journalists' Prize (*Helmut-Sontag-Publizistenpreis*) in 1987 which awards 2,500 Euros annually and is intended to direct the attention of the press and media to librarianship (Helmut Sontag was chairman of the DBV from 1983 – 1986). Publishers and journalists who have promoted librarianship through exceptional, individual reports or through effective continuous, factual reporting in press, radio, television, and the Internet are honored with this prize. The winner and the awards celebration are documented annually in the DBV Yearbook (*DBV-Jahrbuch*).

The City Library "Heinrich Heine" of Halberstadt (*Stadtbibliothek "Heinrich Heine" Halberstadt*) (Saxony-Anhalt) moved into a former chapel in the 600-year-old Petershof on the Domplatz in the year 2000 and in the same year was selected as the "Library of the Year". In its 1,770 sqm, it presents approximately 88,000 media items. The high rooms offer the possibility of including mezzanines and thus expanding the amount of space available for use.

Struktur des Berufsverbandes BIB

Jährliche Mitgliederversammlung

Vorstand
1 Vorsitz., 4 Stellvertr.
Amtsperiode: 3 Jahre

15 Landesgruppen
3-5 köpfiger Vorstand

5 Kommissionen
4-5 Mitglieder

1 beruf. Hrsg.

Baden-Württemberg, Bayern, Berlin, Brandenburg, Hamburg, Hessen, NRW ...

- Komm. Aus- und Fortbildung
- Komm. Eingruppierung u. Besoldung
- Komm. Neue Technologien
- Komm. One-Person-Libraries
- Komm. zur Information von Fachangestellten und Assistenten

Weitere Zuständigkeiten und Aufgaben:
BuB-Herausgeber, Finanzen, AG Lektoratskooperation, BDB-Vorstand, BDB-Plattform Öffentliche Bibliothek, EBLIDA, IFLA-Nationalkomitee, Börsenverein etc.

Verbandszeitschrift "BuB"

2 gewählte Hrsg.

- 3 fest angestellte Redakteure
- 3 Herausgeber
- 10 köpfiger Redaktionsbeirat

Structure of the German Libraries Association (BIB)
English terms for diagram p. 12

With their project "German Internet Library" (*Deutsche Internet-Bibliothek – DIB*), the DBV, the Bertelsmann Foundation, and the SISIS Informationssysteme GmbH introduced an annotated catalog of links with a country-wide email reference service to the Internet public. Special Internet reviewers from 70 contributing libraries in Germany participate in updating this collection of recommendable Internet resources, which is arranged in 20 subject categories. Currently, approximately 8000 quality-approved sites have been listed.

For the first time in the year 2000, the DBV designation of excellence, "Library of the Year" (*Bibliothek des Jahres*), could be awarded with financial support in cooperation with the "*ZEIT*-Foundation of Ebelin and Gerd Bucerius" (*Zeit-Stiftung Ebelin und Gerd Bucerius'*). The national library prize, endowed with 25,000 Euros, recognizes exemplary library work at all levels and is intended to motivate libraries to compete in terms of quality, creativity, and innovation. The prize-winning library is selected by an independent jury, which also has members from the Federal Government, the Standing Conference of Cultural Ministers (KMK), the German Congress of Towns (*Deutscher Städtetag*), and the DBV, among others. The prize is awarded

on October 24, the "Day of the Libraries" (*Tag der Bibliotheken*).

Berufsverband Information Bibliothek e.V. (BIB) (Professional Association Information Library)

The Professional Association Information Library (*Berufsverband Information Bibliothek e.V. – BIB*) emerged in the year 2000 from the convergence of the formerly independent personal associations, the Association of Librarians and Library Assistants (*Verein der Bibliothekare und Assistenten e.V. – VBA*), and the Association of Certified Librarians at Academic and Research Libraries (*Verein der Diplom-Bibliothekare an wissenschaftlichen Bibliotheken e.V. – VdDB, founded in1948*). The VBA developed in 1997 out of the fusion of the Association of Librarians at Public Libraries (*Verein der Bibliothekare an Öffentlichen Bibliotheken e.V. – VBB, founded in 1949*) with the National Association of Library Assistants and other Staff in Libraries (*Bundesverein der Bibliotheksassistent/innen und Assistenten und anderer Mitarbeiter/innen an Bibliotheken e.V. – BBA, founded in 1987*).

Today, the BIB comprises approximately 7300 members and is thus the largest of the two personal librarian associations. It does not see itself as a trade union organization, but nevertheless its focus is the professional representation of its members' interests as the center of its activities. More specifically, efforts are made for the improvement, modernization, and standardization of the training programs; the creation and integration of a modern professional image; issues of achieving competitive salaries and professional levels which adequately reflect the level of training; and staff qualification through targeted continuing education measures. The areas of activity are, for instance, planning and structural issues of librarianship, maintaining national and international contacts, management topics, or the planning and execution – together with the VDB – of the German Librarians' Conference (*Deutscher Bibliothekartag*) which

is the second largest professional librarians subject conference in Germany, second only to the German Library Congress.

An associational commitee (*Vereinsausschuss*) assists the five-person national board of the BIB (*Bundesvorstand*). In this committee, the 15 state groups (*Landesgruppen*), the board and the commissions each send their representatives. Protection of the minority prohibits that a majority of individual professional groups could take over the board. Important constitutional changes can only be enacted if a three-quarters majority is reached. The main office of the Association is in Reutlingen. Important publications from the last years are:

· *Arbeitsvorgänge in wissenschaftlichen Bibliotheken : Beschreibung und Bewertung nach dem Bundes-Angestelltentarifvertrag / BAT* (2000) (Working Procedures in Academic and Research Libraries : Description and Evaluation according to the Federal Employees' Wage Agreement)
· *Allgemeine Systematik für öffentliche Bibliotheken (ASB)* (1999) (General Classification for Public Libraries)
· *Arbeitsvorgänge in öffentlichen Bibliotheken : Beschreibung und Bewertung nach dem Bundes-Angestelltentarifvertrag / BAT* (1999) (Working Procedures in Public Libraries: Description and Evaluation According to the Federal Employees' Wage Agreement)

Every two years, the BIB publishes the Yearbook of Public Libraries (*Jahrbuch der Öffentlichen Bibliotheken*) which serves as an important address book. In addition, since 1949 the Association has published the professional library journal *BuB: Forum für Bibliothek und Information* (*BuB: Forum for Library and Information*) which today has a circulation of approximately 9,000.

Verein Deutscher Bibliothekare e.V. (VDB)

The Association of German Librarians (*Verein Deutscher Bibliothekare e.V.* (VDB)), founded in 1900, is the association of academic and research librarians at the senior level (*höherer Dienst*) with approximately 1,600 members. Its goal is to maintain the continuity among academic and research librarians and to represent their professional interests, to serve the exchange and expansion of their professional skills, and to promote academic and research

librarianship. It is divided into regional associations according to *Land* (*Landesverbände*) and supports four Commissions for professional qualifications, legal issues, the work of the subject specialists, and the cooperation with the BIB Commission for Management and Workplace Control.

Until the mid-1970's, the VDB supported the main professional library work on a national basis in the Federal Republic of Germany; at that time, the DBV or more specifically the DBI, then took over such national tasks and the VDB became more of a purely professional association. One of the major areas of emphasis in the work of this Association is the certification of the qualifications of new librarians. The VDB has repeatedly taken a position on the practical and theoretical education and training of academic and research librarians and has published its recommendations.

The Association's publication is the *Zeitschrift für Bibliothekswesen und Bibliographie – ZfBB*. Its most important publication is the *Jahrbuch der deutschen Bibliotheken*, which was first published in 1902, and is published today every two years. It contains a section with details and statistical data on academic and research libraries, and a second section on people – hence also fulfilling the function of a membership directory.

Since the beginning of the 20th century, the VDB organizes the annual German Librarians' Conference (*Deutschen Bibliothekartag*) as the main professional conference. Since 1952, it has been organized in conjunction with the VdDB, and as of 2001 together with the BIB. The most important conference presentations are published regularly in the *ZfBB* in an independent series which appears separately as a "Sonderheft" of the *ZfBB*.

ekz-Library Service, Reutlingen

Among the central institutions of German librarianship, the *ekz*-Library Service, Inc. (*ekz-bibliotheksservice GmbH – ekz*) , founded in 1947 in Reutlingen, has a unique position. It is a competitive business enterprise serving only libraries and it works under the legal form of a society with limited liability. The 73 partners are, however, exclusively regional corporate bodies of public law: *Länder*, cities, and counties. The *ekz* is one of the founding members of the BDB.

The *ekz* contributes to the further development of libraries through the sales of products and services especially produced for libraries in the areas of collection development, classification and preservation, interior decorating, equipment and furnishings, and organization of libraries. Although for decades, the *ekz* focused on the public libraries in the Federal Republic of Germany, in the last several years there has been a complete and significant change; from a business with an original emphasis on books and furniture, at the beginning of the 21st century, the *ekz* has become a commercial service vendor for all library areas with a comprehensive spectrum of media, service, and consulting offers for all of Europe and a leading company in central Europe in the area of library and media sales with a variety of offerings. Through further services such as sponsoring, continuing professional education activities, and raising staff qualifications for various professional segments, the *ekz* has adapted itself to the current market demands and has developed new marketing areas with a high degree of economic success.

The particular objective of the *ekz* business lies in making a complete offer for everything potentially needed by a library, which can be put together modularly from its diverse individual products. With its bibliographic and classification services, the *ekz* is increasingly moving into the foreground as a data center for public libraries. An Online Ordering Service accelerates the acquisition of available media, whereby the title entries can be transferred via network in machine readable format to the purchasing library. All products can be viewed on the Internet via its homepage, and both searches and orders, as well as information questions and contacting *ekz*, are possible through electronic means. The library readers' department of the *ekz* cooperates in producing the "Book Review Services" (*Lektoratsdienste*) and (*ID-Informationsdienste*, etc.) in context of the *ekz* partnership (*Lektoratskooperation*) with the German Library As-

Among the most important services of the *ekz-bibliotheksservice GmbH in Reutlingen* (Baden-Württemberg) are still the bookbinding offers such as the traditional *ekz* binding, the ekz foil binding, and the *ekz* special binding for paperbacks. The machine for fully automated plastic covering for books, which is unique and was especially constructed for the *ekz*, was first used in production in 1995. It can process 3,000 books per day.

sociation (*Deutschen Bibliotheksverband e.V. –* DBV) and the *Berufsverband Information Bibliothek* e.V. – BIB.

In the recent past, the *ekz* not only furnished many public libraries, but also a rising number of academic and research libraries, among them the *Die Deutsche Bibliothek* in Frankfurt/Main where it has provided the open stacks. In addition, it has been able to realize a series of projects to equip libraries in other European countries.

A remarkable result of the "complete library services" is the possibility for a financial body supporting the library to operate the library together with the *ekz* in the form of a company with limited liability (*Bibliotheks-GmbH*). Until now, there have been only two examples of this. Since 1996 in Schriesheim (Baden-Württemberg) and since 2000 in Siegburg (North Rhine-Westphalia), city libraries exist as companies with limited liability ("*GmbH*"). With these two examples, future-oriented models of privatized public libraries with shared responsibility for their finances have been developed in addition to the City Library of Gütersloh GmbH, which was initiated in 1984 by the Bertelsmann Foundation and has been supported since then by the Foundation and the City of Gütersloh.

The *ekz* has forged new paths in the projects developed for *e-Learning* since 2000 together with the Bertelsmann Foundation: Using the name "bib-web," a series of online self-teaching courses for library personnel were developed for the first time. The first three continuing education courses on the topic of the Internet are modularly structured and build on one another. Several thousand library staff members have completed this course with the final certification (*Abschlusszertifizierung*); additional courses on the topics "Focus Patron: User-Orientation in Libraries" (*Focus Kunde: Nutzerorientierung in Bibliotheken*) and "Library Services for Youth" (*Bibliotheksangebote für Jugendliche*) have expanded the palette of e-learning offerings as of 2002.

The Bertelsmann Foundation, Gütersloh

As the largest private foundation in Germany, the *Bertelsmann Foundation (Bertelsmann Stiftung)* in Gütersloh commissions, among other things, projects in areas affecting public libraries. The Bertelsmann Foundation is very active in the topical areas of "Culture and Education," "Business and Social Aspects," "Democracy and Citizens in Society," "International Understanding," and "Health." Since its establishment by Reinhard Mohn in the year 1977, the Bertelsmann Foundation has, as an operating foundation, assigned itself the task of developing model solutions for societal problems and issues for the future. Since that time, more than 180 projects have been completed. The Foundation is valued well beyond the borders of the Federal Republic of Germany by decision makers in politics and administration, business and society, as a practice-oriented "Workshop for Reform" and as

Bertelsmann Stiftung

a catalyst for modernization of state and administration. To accomplish this, the Bertelsmann Foundation follows the principles of practicality, orientation to patron needs, innovation, sustainability, building partnerships, and evaluation.

Since the beginning of its activities, the Bertelsmann Foundation has promoted and supported public libraries in order to develop and test out cooperative solutions for the societal challenges of the future. So that these strategies obtain a model character, the Foundation places great value on practical testing in context of projects being conducted with partners in Germany and in other countries, such as Spain, Egypt and Poland. Furthermore, innovative methods, discoveries, and practical experience from the countries with the leading libraries of the world are collected in an international network, exchanged, developed, and expanded. In doing so, new strategies for solving the problems flow in from other areas and contribute to anchoring businesslike thinking and behavior in libraries.

In the meantime, numerous "tried and true" projects, tested in practice, have been developed for the library area. This concerns, for instance, issues of consistent service orientation, of modern presentation of library collections and library furnishings, systematic promotion of reading, or strat-

The newly erected City Library of Gütersloh (*Stadtbibliothek Gütersloh*) (North Rhein-Westphalia) was built in 1983 with support of the *Bertelsmann Stiftung* and was the first public library using the legal form of a company with limited liability (*Gesellschaft mit beschränkter Haftung – GmbH*). 110,000 media are available in approximately 2,500 sqm. In the center of the three-storey library, directly behind the circulation desk, a readers' café invites guests for refreshment.

egies for effective management and organization of libraries. Modern library work must be flexible, oriented to the target user groups, and future-oriented, transparent to the external world, and able to undergo performance evaluations. These are the maxims of the Foundation. Long-term projects, such as "Public Libraries in Organizational Comparison" and "BIX – The Library Index", take these maxims into account. The comparison of the operational data of libraries serves as a framework for the goal of defining individual positions in terms of self-evaluation and creates the basis for effective improvement. Since 2003, these considerations have been expanded to include data on academic and research libraries.

In order to further qualify library personnel as navigators in the world-wide flood of information and data, the Bertelsmann Foundation cooperated with the *ekz Bibliotheksservice GmbH* to develop the online training program called *"bibweb"* – a training program for using the Internet for librarians with three successive learning modules building on one another; it provides library personnel with a practice-oriented instrument for training and continuing education to raise their Internet competencies. In 2002, the Foundation, in cooperation with the BDB, began the two-year project "Library 2007" (*"Bibliothek 2007"*).

The Goethe Institute Inter Nationes e.V., Munich and Bonn

By virtue of its commission from the State, the *Goethe Institute Inter Nationes e.V.* (GIIN) takes on duties of foreign cultural and educational politics. To achieve this, the GIIN pursues three major goals: maintaining (and expanding) international cultural cooperation, promoting skills in the German language abroad, and communicating a comprehensive image of Germany through information on cultural, social and political life in Germany.

Today 125 cultural institutes of the GIIN in 77 countries conduct cultural programs, offer language courses, support teachers, universities and official bodies in promoting the German language and offer current information about Germany. In

Germany itself, 16 Goethe Institutes offer language courses using the most modern teaching methods for more than 25,000 foreign participants annually. International cultural journals, books, informative materials on Germany, entertainment and documentary films, and various differentiated online offerings are made available to interested persons in the entire world. The visitors' program provides informational trips to Germany led by experts for 1,500 foreign multipliers from the press, media, and culture annually.

The Goethe Institute Inter Nationes has been very active over the last several years in the area of information and library work with the objective of promoting professional dialogue on differing concepts, methods, and application of information and knowledge management, of library organization, and training and continuing education on an international level. The most important tasks of the information and library work of the Goethe Institute Inter Nationes are:

· *Library cooperation:* In order to promote professional communication in the areas of the book, media, and libraries, professional conferences, workshops, study trips, training and continuing education events, etc., are organized in conjunction with institutions in the host country
· *Promoting Literature and Translations:* The cultural institutes abroad mediate German-language literature, promote its translation, and for this purpose, work closely with the press, publishers, book trade, and libraries in the host countries
· *Qualified Information Advising:* (Reference Service) Fundamental components of the international work of the Goethe Institute Inter Nationes include providing information on developments, events, publications, and development of thematic multimedia services relating to German culture and German current events for selected target groups.
· *Information Management:* The GIIN simultaneously maintains high-level, current offerings of media which are customized to the local needs, and effective, reliable services, not only for the libraries and information centers in the foreign Institutes, but also for numerous foreign partner libraries, for instance, in more than 50 German reading rooms in foreign libraries.

The Goethe Institute Inter Nationes with its central offices in Munich and Bonn is not a state institu-

**GOETHE INSTITUT
INTER NATIONES**

tion, but a society which receives Federal subsidies on the basis of a basic contract with the Foreign Affairs Office. Founded in 1951, the Goethe Institute was combined in the year 2001 with Inter Nationes (founded in 1952), the largest intermediary organization for German cultural and educational politics abroad with some 3,000 staff members around the world.

National Cooperation with other Cultural Information and Documentation Areas

Imperative for positive, continued development of librarianship in Germany is the close cooperation on all levels with partners from cultural, information and documentation areas, comprising, among others, the German Literature Conference (*Deutsche Literaturkonferenz*), the Reading Foundation (*Stiftung Lesen*), the Association of the German Book Trade (*Börsenverein des Deutschen Buchhandels*) or the German Council on Culture (*Deutscher Kulturrat*), and certainly last but not least, the German Association for Information Science and Information Practice (*Deutsche Gesellschaft für Informationswissenschaft und Informationspraxis – DGI*).

The German Association for Information Science and Information Practice (*Deutsche Gesellschaft für Informationswissenschaft und Informationspraxis e.V – DGI*), founded in1948 as the German Association for Documentation (*Deutsche Gesellschaft für Dokumentation*), is an academic and professional learned society for the advancement of research, teaching and practice in the area of information and documentation, with its main office in Frankfurt/Main. This Association develops subject-oriented foundations and working methods, maintains cooperation with national and international institutions, and pursues the application of new technologies including the legal issues connected with them. The professional journal of this Association is *Information – Wissenschaft und Praxis* (= Information – Science and Practice). The cooperation partners of the DGI are the Discussion Group Computer Science (*Gesprächskreis Informatik – GKI*), the Information and Communication Initiative of the German Learned Societies (*IuK-Initiative der wissenschaftlichen Fachgesellschaften in Deutschland – IuK*), the German Information Network (GIN), and the European Council of Information Associations (ECIA).

The annual conferences "German Documentalist Conferences" (*Deutsche Dokumentartage*) show the breadth and variation of the content dealt with in the documentalist profession and treat among other items, technical developments and management issues, as well as markets and marketing possibilities in the information and documentation area. In the year 2000 for the first time, the DGI and BDB jointly organized the Congress as the 90th Librarians' and the 52nd Documentalist Conference in Leipzig with the theme "Information and the Public." This Congress made very clear how much the work profile and the objectives of both associations had converged over time and that they will have to move even more closely together in the future.

International Cooperation

At the end of the 20th century, as a result of the political developments in Europe, numerous competencies for German librarianship shifted to European institutions and groups. Questions regarding copyright, lending rights, taxation law, the formation of consortia, and issues of international interlibrary loan and problems of providing data connections (Euro-ISDN) are decided at the European level, or even in part at a global level.

In light of world-wide electronic networking and advancing integration of research and information mediation, German libraries, as in all other countries, are dependent on international cooperation.

The context for such cooperation is offered by a series of international organizations in which German institutions and experts actively participate.

The German librarian associations and societies are members of the International Federation of Library Associations and Institutions (IFLA), the umbrella organization for libraries, founded in 1927 in Glasgow. The IFLA maintains a central Headquarters in the rooms of the Dutch Royal Library in The Hague.

To coordinate German participation in the IFLA, the *IFLA National Committee* was formed in 1974. Today, in addition to the member associations of the BDB, the German Special Libraries Association (*Arbeitsgemeinschaft Spezialbibliotheken – ASpB*) and the Association of Libraries of the State of North Rhein-Westphalia (*Verband der Bibliotheken des Landes Nordrhein-Westfalen – VdBNW*) also *Die Deutsche Bibliothek*, the State Libraries in Berlin and Munich, the Saxonian State Library – State and University Library of Dresden (*Sächsische Landesbibliothek – Staats- und Universitätsbibliothek Dresden*), as well as the German Research Council (*Deutsche Forschungsgemeinschaft – DFG*), are represented. The DFG is the host and supports the IFLA membership of the associations with financial subsidies.

On the European level, the German library associations are represented through the *European Bureau of Library Information and Documentation Associations* (EBLIDA) which was founded in 1991 – also in the Hague – as a representative unit for the interests of libraries and information services at the European Parliament, at the European Commission and at the Council of Europe. The goal of the EBLIDA Bureau is to further continuous library political lobby work through information exchange and professional advisory activities and communication with the representatives and parliamentarians.

Maintaining contacts is of considerable significance for the EBLIDA Bureau, especially for the harmonization of the EU legal regulations which become law in all the EU member states. At the center of EDLIBA activities during the last years are professional recommendations regarding the proposed guidelines for the harmonization of copyright and the related protection rights for intellectual property in the information society. In addition, as a mediator between national and European bodies, the Bureau executes projects for advancing copyright,

licensing and library politics for public libraries with financial support of the EU. The expanded possibilities for EU support, which has been increasing especially for libraries, will contribute to the preservation of cultural diversity of the member countries and their regions, and to guarantee national identities. Naturally, economic points of view also play a role here. The library program of the European Commission, through which innovative techniques are promoted, was first embedded in the "Telematics" program until it was detached from the Information Society Program in 1998, in which the area of "Digital Heritage and Cultural Content" was especially important and meaningful for libraries.

At the European level, the individual national libraries work together in the *Conference of European National Librarians* (CENL). As result of this cooperation, the information service called *Gabriel* (Gateway to Europe's National Libraries) was formed, providing comprehensive information on collections, tasks, and activities of all European national libraries and access to their homepages and online catalogs. This multimedia Internet service, which is free of charge, is regarded as an important step in creating a virtual European library.

Under the sponsorship of the Council of Europe, an international coalition of academic and research libraries founded LIBER (*Ligue des Bibliothèques européennes de recherche = League of European Research Libraries*) in 1971, in which numerous German state libraries (*Landesbibliotheken*), regional libraries and libraries of higher education institutions are members. At the same time, LIBER possesses advisory status at the Council of Europe and is intended to help the academic and research libraries in Europe to form a functioning network across national borders and thus secure the preservation of the European cultural heritage, improve access to collections in European libraries, and establish more efficient information services in Europe. LIBER also supports measures and projects for improving professional qualifications of library personnel through conferences, seminars, task forces and publications.

5 COOPERATION AMONG GERMAN LIBRARIES

Cooperation within Local, Regional and National Services

Intensive and successful cooperation within the German library system is by no means a recent phenomenon. Its roots go back to Prussia at the beginning of the 20th century and the tradition was to be continued later in the "German Empire." The economic problems caused by First World War and the immense losses wreaked by the Second had already led librarians to seek new areas of cooperative effort. However, it was not until the expansion in the educational sector during the 1960's and the vast increase in demands for literature provision and information services that any attempt was made to introduce a measure of rational planning into the development of the German library system. The introduction of data processing and the expansion of electronic networks gave new impetus to the idea of cooperation and made it clear that the age of the Digital Library was dawning.

The Principles of Library Cooperation

In 1964 the Academic Council *(Wissenschaftsrat)*, the highest respected advisory body in academic research and technology, published its "Recommendations for the Development of Academic and Research Libraries" (*Empfehlungen zum Ausbau der wissenschaftlichen Bibliotheken*). These encompassed not only fundamental ideas on the future structure of the academic library system in the contemporary Federal Republic, but also concrete recommendations for 82 individual libraries and budgeting models for university libraries. Furthermore, the recommendations set the ball rolling on impor-

In 1992 the State Library of Lower Saxony and University Library of Göttingen (*Niedersächsische Staats- und Universitätsbibliothek Göttingen*) moved into a modern building (architect: Gerber and Partner), enabling 1.5 million of its 4.5 million volumes to be placed on open access. The Library has assumed responsibility for several national functions, including the administration of around 20 special subject collections, and is advancing confidently on the road towards the Digital Library. In 2002 it was chosen as "Library of the Year" by the DBV for its outstanding achievements.

tant projects, such as the establishment of textbook collections and the creation of inner-university union catalogs. They also encouraged the development both of overall planning concepts and of individual measures, such as models for the assessment of budget, staff and space requirements.

Lacking a central agency responsible for the German library system in its entirety, the German Library Conference *(Deutsche Bibliothekskonferenz)*, at that time the top-level organization in academic and public libraries, acted on its own initiative and produced the structural development plan *Bibliotheksplan '73*. As its subtitle indicates, the plan was intended as an "outline plan for the development of a comprehensive library network in the Federal Republic of Germany." It assumed that the "continually increasing demands made on all areas of general education, vocational training, teaching, and research" could only be met "if all forms of literature, which will continue to form the basis for learning in the future, are made available together with other information sources to everyone, everywhere". The only way of achieving this goal, it was concluded, was through the unification of the library system and the cooperative efforts of all the libraries involved.

The present formal basis of interlibrary cooperation is the position paper *Bibliotheken '93*, (= "Libraries '93"), compiled by librarians from all over Germany and published by the Federation of German Library Associations (*Bundesvereinigung Deutscher Bibliotheksverbände*) in 1993. It includes all types of libraries and has at last succeeded in breaking down the traditional barriers between the two opposing public and academic library poles. As in the previous plan, *Bibliotheken '73*, each type and size of library is assigned its individual place in the literature provision network, this position defining the library's aims, which in their turn determine the scope of the resources required. Functions of a global nature are best carried out by central agencies or organized on a cooperative interlibrary basis.

The necessity for joint action has been rendered more urgent by the decentralized structure of the German library system, the wide variety of funding bodies, the political and administrative framework of the Federal state, the absence of a national planning and management authority, and many other factors. *Cooperation* has become a constitutional feature of the German library system, as can be

Building 1 of the Berlin State Library – Prussian Cultural Heritage houses the Historical Research Library with literature published up until 1955, while Building 2 accommodates the Lending and Reference Library for recent literature published from 1956 onwards. The General Reading Room (shown above), providing a reference collection of 90,000 works on four floors is complemented by four additional subject specialist reading rooms: the Manuscript, Eastern European, Cartography, and Oriental and East Asian Reading Rooms. The users are primarily students.

demonstrated by the large number of collaborative projects and the many interlibrary working groups and associations.

This points to the fact that the unusual structure of the German library system is by no means a disadvantage, but can, on the contrary, deliver impressive results if responsibilities are shared and cooperation properly planned. Nevertheless, cooperation is no compensation for deficient funding and no alternative to the establishment of central coordinating bodies.

There are two kinds of functions particularly suited to cooperative methods: those of national significance for which a division of labor is dictated by the sheer scope of their aims and objectives, and those of a repetitive nature, affecting a large number of libraries and thus lending themselves to cooperative rationalization. There are, therefore, opportunities for cooperation at local, regional or national levels, or again in a European or international dimension. Many German libraries are engaged on cross-border projects and associative schemes, for example in the Baltic countries (Bibliotheca Baltica), the Alpine region (ARGE Alp), the Upper Rhine area

The new building of the State Library of Baden (*Badische Landesbibliothek*) in Karlsruhe (Baden-Württemberg, architect: Oswald Mathias Ungers), completed in 1991, radiates severity and assertive timelessness. The geometric center of the building is the main reading room, featuring a dome in the style of the reading rooms of the 19th century. Within EUCOR (The European Confederation of Upper Rhine Universities) the *Badische Landesbibliothek* works together with other academic libraries in the region.

(EUCOR) or in the EUREGIO Maas-Rhine area. They are involved in the work of international organizations and committees, including being members of the IFLA. German libraries also participate in the various initiatives and development programs of the European Union and in the activities of UNESCO. In the following examples, however, the emphasis is on inner-German projects of particular importance and national significance.

Acquisitions Cooperation

Academic libraries have for many decades worked closely together in the field of acquisitions. There have also been isolated cases of cooperative acquisition projects In the public library sector too; for example, the large city libraries of North Rhine-Westphalia have agreed among themselves on the allocation of special acquisition responsibility for particular subject areas, with *Land* funding. The projects described below are concerned with specific collection development. However, an increasing proportion of acquisition funds is being used for the purchase of usage rights. Like their counterparts abroad, German libraries have formed consortia for the cooperative licensing of electronic media. Particularly in the case of high-priced digital products, consortial agreements enable libraries to increase the number of titles on offer without overextending their acquisitions budgets.

The German Research Council and the Special Subject Area Collection Program

The German Research Council (*Deutsche Forschungsgemeinschaft,* DFG) is the central autonomous body appointed to promote research in universities and publicly-funded research institutions in Germany. It serves all academic disciplines by financing research projects and encouraging collaboration among researchers. The DFG was founded in 1949 to carry on the tradition initiated by the Emergency Council of German Science *(Notgemeinschaft der Deutschen Wissenschaft)* in 1920. For this purpose the DFG receives grants from the central *Bund* and the regional *Länder*, and to a small extent from private sources. The basis for the state grants is the "Framework Agreement on the Advancement of Research" (*Rahmenvereinbarung Forschungsförderung),* established under Article 91 b of the Basic Law (*Grundgesetz*).

Since academic libraries form an important part of the research infrastructure, they too receive support from the DFG, amounting in 2002 to around

31 million Euros. These funding measures are centered on national projects in the following areas: National literature provision, whereby large libraries agree to acquire the literature of a particular subject area, these subject areas being combined with the resources of special libraries within a network of virtual libraries; new publication forms and procedures, including measures to ensure the long-term availability of digital documents; information systems management in universities and research institutions; cultural transfer in research information systems including the long-term availability of non-digital documents. These fields include projects on the acquisition and provision of research literature, on the development of a Distributed Digital Research Library (Verteilte digitale Forschungsbibliothek) and subject-based networks, on the indexing of literature and source material, and on book preservation measures.

National literature provision forms the core of the DFG´s library support program and involves at the present three types of libraries: universal libraries with special subject collection areas, special research libraries, and the Central Subject Libraries. Building on the 19th century model, the DFG developed a Special Subject Area Collection Program (Sondersammelgebietsplan) for the academic and research library system. The Program was drawn up to ensure that even during the difficult years of reconstruction following the Second World War at least one copy of every essential foreign work of research literature would be available in Germany. Over time, the program developed into a fully-fledged national literature provision system serving the interests of the scientific and research community.

Over 40 of Germany's most efficient state, university and special libraries share a clearly-defined system of around 120 subject or regionally-oriented special acquisition fields. Following reunification, the former exclusively West German system was expanded; new subject areas were created and existing fields reallocated to include libraries in the former East German region. The task of the participating libraries is to build special subject collections in their allocated fields on a systematic basis and to make these available nationwide with the help of DFG funding. The subject field definitions are broad and include all forms of information media. To increase the system's efficiency, subject area libraries are expected to include digital publications in their acquisitions profile. Since the objective of the Special Subject Area Collection Program is to make

The Saxonian State Library and University Library Dresden (Sächsische Landesbibliothek – Staats- und Universitätsbibliothek Dresden) was able to house all of its previously separate departments (special collections, textbook collection, the German Photo Library (Deutsche Photothek) in its new building opened in 2002 (design: Ortner and Ortner). Readers have a choice of 900 work spaces, 200 of which are in the large Reading Room. In 1993, the Saxonian State Library took on the DFG special subject area of "Contemporary Post-War Art."

provision for future research literature require-ments, as well as to consider present needs, a solu-tion will have to be found to the problem of long-term availability of digital material.

Information on the DFG Special Subject Areas and the libraries to which they have been assigned, can be obtained from a number of reference works, or alternatively on the Internet via WEBIS, a web-based information system. While the demands of the main disciplines medicine, science and tech-nology, and economics are met by the Central Sub-ject Libraries, the remaining subject areas are di-vided among a large number of universal and spe-cial libraries. These are responsible either for indi-vidual subject fields, such as botany, forestry, psy-chology and theology, or for linguistic, cultural or geographical regions, such as Southern Africa, South Asia and Oceania or the languages of the Indian and Eskimo peoples.

The literature acquired under the national litera-ture provision program is cataloged, subject-in-dexed and recorded in the regional and national union catalogs. In addition, it may be disseminated to interested researchers in the form of special con-ventional or electronic publications, such as new acquisitions lists or periodical contents indexes. Al-though this literature was formerly made available through the German interlibrary loan service, many subject area libraries, alongside the Central Subject Libraries, now offer swift document delivery directly to the user, using electronic ordering and dispatch. The digitalization of the special subject area collec-tion will enjoy top priority status in the future and is another method of making these holdings more easily available.

Since 1998, the Special Subject Area Collection Libraries (*Sammelschwerpunktbibliotheken*) have been developed with the financial support of the DFG into "Virtual Subject Libraries" and amalgam-ated into a "Distributed Digital Research Library." The Virtual Subject Libraries provide access to high-quality Internet sources and other documents per-taining to their individual subject area. Since 1999, The Federal Ministry of Education and Research (*Bundesministerium für Bildung und Forschung –* BMBF*)* has promoted the parallel creation of infor-mation networks designed to link bibliographical records with their matching electronic full text sources. In order that researchers and students may have clearly-organized access to the wealth of in-

The historical Reading Room of Tübingen University Library in Baden-Württemberg (*Universitätsbibliothek Tübingen*), built in 1912 (architect: Paul Bonatz) is graced by a large mural depicting the struggle be-tween the present and the wisdom of the past. The Tübingen University Library, founded in 1477, is part of a two-layered system and is responsible for several broad subject areas from the DFG´s Special Subject Area Collection Program (*Sondersammelgebiets-programm*), including theology.

formation resources available both on the Internet and in conventional form, both projects are being combined under a common portal.

The Collection of German Imprints (*Sammlung Deutscher Drucke)*

While the large national libraries of other countries house comprehensive collections of their own na-tional literature, Germany first started a central archive of printed German culture with the found-ing of the *Deutsche Bücherei* in 1913. The member libraries of the Working Group on the Collection of German Imprints (*Arbeitsgemeinschaft Sammlung Deutscher Drucke)* have set themselves the task of systematically completing the fragmentary records of materials published in German-speaking coun-tries up until 1912. From 1913 onwards the *Deutsche Bibliothek* and the *Deutsche Bücherei* have been able to continue the *Sammlung Deutscher Drucke* together on the basis of their legal deposit copies. It has thus been possible to create an increasingly complete virtual national library.

Acquisition responsibilities have been divided among the participating libraries on a chronological basis. The individual segments have been allocated to those libraries already possessing substantial holdings of the period in question. The six member libraries of the Working Group are responsible for the following periods:

1450 – 1600: Bavarian State Library, Munich
1601 – 1700: Herzog August Library, Wolfenbüttel
1701 – 1800: State Library of Lower Saxony and University Library of Göttingen
1801 – 1870: City and University Library and Senckenberg Library in Frankfurt am Main
1871 – 1912: State Library Berlin – Prussian Cultural Heritage
1913 pres.: Die Deutsche Bibliothek

Each of the member libraries acquires for its allocated period all printed material published in German-speaking countries and all material in the German language, regardless of where it was published. Priority is given to the purchase of imprints not yet available in a freely-accessible German library. All printed materials acquired through the project are registered in the supraregional catalog databases and can thus be searched worldwide on the Internet. In many cases, the historical imprints are in need of special preservation measures; in addition, the question of filming or digitalizing the document may also have to be considered.

Even though around 80,000 works have been acquired in the original print form and more than 40,000 on microfilm, the development of this *virtual national library* still has a long way to go. It is impossible to say how many books have been published in Germany since the invention of letter-press printing. Estimates have indicated that several more

The *Herzog August Bibliothek in Wolfenbüttel* (Lower Saxony) was founded in 1572 by Duke August and by the 17th century was one of the largest collections of literature in Europe. Today it is a center for research and study of European cultural history. The core collection, containing about 135,000 titles, is housed in the antique Augusteerhalle of the Bibliotheca Augusta (built 1884–1887), the central building of the Wolfenbüttel library complex.

decades of collection at the present level will be necessary, making the *Sammlung Deutscher Drucke* a project of monumental dimensions.

Book Review Cooperation in Public Libraries (*Lektoratskooperation*)

The *Lektoratskooperation* (LK), an inestimable aid to collection development in public libraries, was initiated in 1976 and aims to reduce duplicate effort in the task of choosing books and audiovisual media. Its main objective is to aid public libraries in evaluating the more than 85,000 new media published every year in Germany and to help them decide which titles to order.

The *Lektoratskooperation* combines the advantages of a decentralized, practice-oriented market evaluation system with the efficiency of a centrally-organized reviewing resource. Participatory bodies are the German Library Association (*Deutscher Bibliotheksverband)* with around 75 subject specialists (*Lektoren*) in about 60 libraries, the Professional Association Information Libraries (*Berufsverband Information Bibliothek,* BIB) with around 250 reviewers and the library supplier *ekz-bibliotheksservice GmbH,* whose review department has adopted an overall coordinating function.

The *Lektoratskooperation* program in a narrow sense evaluates non-fiction only. Fiction, children's books and youth literature, along with tape and audiovisual media (talking books, videos, CD-ROMs, DVDs) are screened by the staff of the *ekz* and evaluated by the BIB reviewers. The task of the LK staff is to filter out of the mass of new German publications those titles of interest to public libraries and to decide whether these should be evaluated, i.e., annotated by themselves, or whether they should be recommended for more detailed appraisal by one of the BIB reviewers. This information is used to compile a series of review services produced and edited by the *ekz*.

Libraries can subscribe to these evaluation services. The complete, limited, and selected editions of the *ekz Information Service* (*Informationsdienst – ID*) are published weekly. The "full edition" of the *ID*, containing 14,000 titles annually, is aimed at large and medium-sized city library systems with specialized collections. The *ID* "basic edi-

Especially active members of the book evaluation program are the staff of the libraries in the large cities classified under Sections 1 and 2 of the German Library Association categories, (cities with over 100,000 inhabitants). Würzburg City Library in Bavaria, extended in 2001, is responsible for the *Lektoratskooperation* subject area Geography.

tion" with 10,000 titles annually is for the libraries of medium-sized towns with correspondingly smaller acquisition budgets and is identical in content to the *ekz's* parallel monthly publication "BA. Reviews and Annotations" (*BA. Besprechungen und Annotationen*). The "selected edition" of the *ID* contains 6,000 titles per year. The monthly "*ID 3000*" with around 3,000 individually selected appraisals is targeted at public libraries in small towns and communities of less than 10,000 persons. There is a separate monthly "*Medien-Info*" for non-book media listing 3,000 titles annually. In addition, standing order offers by subject and on a sliding financial scale enable libraries to use the *ekz's* central services, an output of the *Lektoratskooperation*, for current collection development at the local level.

Public libraries profit from a subscription to the *ekz Information Service* in several ways. Firstly, they receive recommendations and references they can use to develop their own collections. Secondly, they can take advantage of the *ekz's* other services, such as the cataloging records and subject headings of *Die Deutsche Bibliothek*, or the classification notations of the four most frequently-used public library classification schemes. However, the information services are often criticized for being slow and out of date; in spite of continual improvements and the increasing use of modern communications technology, there are still some organizational weak points in the complex system.

Cooperation among Academic Libraries

Cooperation in the cataloging sector and the exploitation of central services are only possible if participating libraries agree on a common set of cataloging rules. Such rules do indeed exist, in the form of the Descriptive Cataloguing Rules (*Regeln für die alphabetische Katalogisierung – RAK),* widely used in German academic and public libraries, and the Subject Cataloguing Rules (*Regeln für die Schlagwortkatalogisierung – RSWK*), used by many research libraries. These rules are further complemented by various authority files, such as the Common Corporate Names Authority File (*Gemeinsame Körperschaftsdatei – GKD*), the Personal Names Authority File (*Personennamendatei – PND*) and the Subject Headings Authority File (*Schlagwortnormdatei – SWD*). The production of standardized formal rules and the development and maintenance of comprehensive authority files are not only a prerequisite for successful library cooperation, they are also an example of it.

Of course, outside services in the field of formal and subject cataloging can be (and indeed frequently were) utilized in a conventional environment, but they come into their own when combined with data processing. The German Machine-readable Exchange Format for Libraries (*Maschinelles Austauschformat für Bibliotheken – MAB*), developed essentially by *Die Deutsche Bibliothek* in Frankfurt am Main, laid the foundations for the reciprocal use of machine-readable catalog data.

Die Deutsche Bibliothek is the leading supplier of bibliographic services, delivering over 16 million current records per year. Catalog entries for all titles in the various *German National Bibliography* (*Deutsche Nationalbibliographie*) series are generated in compliance with the Descriptive Cataloguing Rules for Academic and Research Libraries (*Regeln für die alphabetische Katalogisierung in wissenschaftlichen Bibliotheken – RAK-WB*) and can be ordered in conventional or electronic form. Subject terms or headings generated in accordance with the *RSWK* have been included since 1986 in all subject-indexed new title records. Plans exist to introduce the Dewey Decimal Classification (DDC) as an additional subject cataloging instrument. Libraries wishing to convert their conventional card catalogs into machine-readable form in order to include older holdings in their online catalogs can use the records of the *German National Bibliography* for all German titles back to 1945, as these have been converted into electronic form and are available on CD-ROM and DVD.

At the end of 2001, the Standardization Committee (*Standardisierungsausschuss*), based at *Die Deutsche Bibliothek*, announced its recommendation to relinquish the German MAB data structure in favor of the American MARC standard, and at the same time to replace the German cataloging rules (RAK) with the *Anglo-American Cataloging Rules (AACR2)*, a recommendation which immediately elicited widespread opposition within the German library system. A feasibility study, funded by the DFG and scheduled for 2005, is to help the Conference of Culture Ministers (*Kulturministerkonferenz*) reach a decision on the changeover.

The Regional Network Systems

The idea behind the regional network systems, created in the 1970s, was that libraries should be able to use data generated by other libraries to facilitate the cataloging of their own new acquisitions. The cooperative exchange of cataloging records, initially limited to descriptive data, but later extended to include subject indexing, had a considerable rationalization effect on book processing. In addition, comprehensive record files were created which proved of inestimable value as search tools in the management of interlibrary lending.

The library networks were originally regionally-based, but have developed over the years into institutions spanning the *Länder* borders. Though initially their main objective was the cooperative development of a common catalog database, the networks have since taken on new responsibilities and expanded their services to become competitors in the information technology market.

Examples of the networks' activities are the maintenance of union catalogs as records of older monograph titles in the region and the later conversion of these catalogs into machine-readable form; the planning and management of the computer-based structures involved in creating a regional network; the implementation of new document delivery systems, the development of digital libraries and the conception of broad training programs. However, their main job remains the maintenance of library computer centers. These centers are responsible for the upkeep of the network's online union catalogs, which the members use as central cataloging and search tools for the supply of data to their local systems.

Today the vast majority of academic libraries are members of one of the regional network systems. At present there are six systems, with responsibility for the respective *Länder* as shown on p. 88.

The computer centers of the network systems employ a variety of software. From the outset, the GBV has used the imported Dutch library system *Pica* in its network center. Other German Pica users are the Hesse Library Network (HeBIS), *Die Deutsche Bibliothek*, and the State Library in Berlin, which in turn collaborates on an international level with OCLC/Pica in Leyden and the *Agence Bibliographique de l'Enseignement Supérieur* (ABES), the French library system based in Montpellier. Two network systems (NRW-BV in the HBV and the KOBV in Berlin-Brandenburg) have chosen ALEPH, a widely-used international system.

In order to reduce the disadvantages of regionally-limited location records for monographs and other non-serial publications, the German Library Institute in Berlin (*Deutsches Bibliotheksinstitut*) combined all the records of the library networks and other individual libraries from 1983 until 1997 to produce the Union Catalog of Machine-readable Catalog Data (*Verbundkatalog Maschinenlesbarer Katalogdaten Deutscher Bibliotheken* – VK). The VK, which was published first on microfiche and later made available as an online database, was a useful instrument in the management and acceleration of interlibrary lending.

In the meantime, the VK has been replaced by new technical solutions. The Karlsruher Virtual Catalog (*Karlsruher Virtueller Katalog* – KVK) links up the regional union catalogs independent of their various software platforms to form a virtual union catalog. Within a single search, it is possible to cover a pool of web-based library and book trade catalogs listing more than 75 million titles. Since 1997 the KVK has grown to become one of the most important search instruments in the Federal Republic and is consulted by over a million users each month. Several similar virtual catalogs based on the idea and technology of the KVK have since been realized by the University Library in Karlsruhe for individual regions (e.g. Rhineland-Palatinate), subject fields (e.g. Orientalia), geographical literature areas (e.g. *Länder* bibliographies) and media types (e.g. videos). In connection with the creation of digital libraries and portals, and with the introduction of cross-network ordering systems, similar search instruments are also being developed and marketed by the regional network systems.

Among these is the Digital Library NRW (DigiBib), developed by the University Library Center in Cologne and with several public libraries among its contributors. The DigiBib enables the user to conduct a search simultaneously in a large number of information sources, including library catalogs and literature databases from all over the world. If the target text is found, the user will be informed whether it is available online, via a document delivery service, in a library or for sale in an online bookshop. If it cannot be retrieved, links will guide the user by subject to online and CD-ROM databases (e.g. dictionaries and subject databases) or to high-quality web sites. At present, the full portal is only available to members of the universities in North Rhine-Westphalia, the Rhineland-Palatinate and the Saarland; others can access it via the guest interface, though with limited content.

The National Periodicals Database (*Zeitschriftendatenbank* – ZDB)

Whereas monograph cataloging is organized decentrally within the library network system, provision was made from the outset for a single coun-

Network Systems and Regions
in Germany

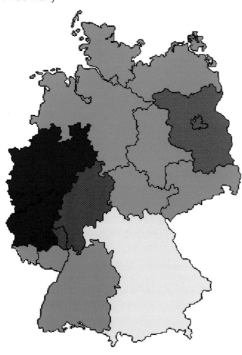

Violet:
Hesse Library Information System, Frankfurt am Main
(*Hessisches Bibliotheks-Informationssystem* – HeBIS)
For the areas of Hesse, Rhine-Hesse (eastern Rhineland-Palatinate)
676 member libraries, 3.2 million titles with 7 million
holdings records

Light blue:
Southwest German Library Network (*Südwestdeut-
scher Bibliotheksverbund* – SWB), Library Service Center Baden-Württemberg (*Bibliotheksservice-Zentrum
Baden-Württemberg* – BSZ), Constance
For the areas of Baden-Württemberg, southern Rhineland-Palatinate), the Saarland, Saxony
1.000 member libraries, 10 million titles with 28 million holdings records

Yellow:
Bavarian Library Network (*Bibliotheksverbund Bayern*
– BVB), Munich
For the area of Bavaria
95 member libraries, 10 million titles with 25 million
holdings records

Green:
Joint Library Network, Göttingen,
(*Gemeinsamer Bibliotheksverbund* – GBV)
For the areas of Bremen, Hamburg, Mecklenburg-
Western-Pomerania, Lower Saxony, Sachsen-Anhalt,
Schleswig-Holstein, Thuringia
430 member libraries, 16 million titles with 38 million
holdings records

Red:
Cooperative Library Network Berlin-Brandenburg
(*Kooperativer Bibliotheksverbund Berlin-Brandenburg*
– KOBV)
For the areas of Berlin, Brandenburg
30 member libraries, 8 million titles with 20 million
holdings records

Dark blue:
North Rhine-Westphalian Library Network
(*Nordrhein-Westfälischer Bibliotheksverbund* –
NRW-BV), University Library Center of the Land NRW,
Cologne (*Hochschulbibliothekszentrum des Landes
NRW* – HBZ)
For the areas of North Rhine-Westphalia, western and
northern Rhineland-Palatinate
900 member libraries, 11 million titles with 22 million
holdings records

trywide system for periodicals. With financial help
from the DFG, the ZDB was established in 1973 as
a cooperative network system into which periodical
titles and location details are entered by the participating libraries. Owing to the high standard of its
bibliographical records, the ZDB has taken on the
role of an authority file agency for the formal cataloging of periodical titles. The original idea of the
allocation of the respective responsibilities for the
editorial and technical domains to two different institutions has been upheld: following the demise of
the DBI at the end of 1999, the State Library in Berlin assumed sole responsibility for the ZDB, whereas
systems administration was transferred from the
DBI to *Die Deutsche Bibliothek*, and so the ZDB
also uses the *Pica* system.

Meanwhile, 4,300 institutions are involved in
the development and upkeep of the ZDB. Around
150 of the larger libraries catalog their periodicals,
series and newspapers directly in the ZDB; the remaining libraries report their titles to one of the
larger libraries or call on the services of the editorial

Search Interface of the Karlsruher Virtual Catalog at www.ubka.uni-karlsruhe.de/kvk.html

Retrieval Interface of the Digital Library NRW at www.digibib.net

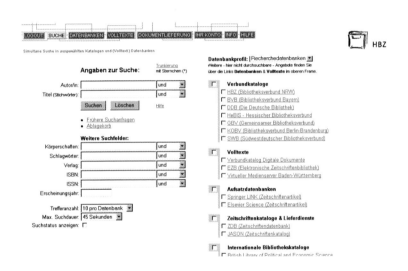

staff, who are also responsible for data consistency and double-entry avoidance. Title and holdings details are passed back to the library networks, so that besides being recorded in the central ZDB they are also listed in the regional databases and local online catalogs. In addition, the *SUBITO* system is regularly updated with the latest ZDB data.

Today the ZDB contains almost 1.1 million serials titles, 400,000 of which are current periodicals, and nearly 5.7 million locations. As the vast majority of institute and other special libraries do not make the periodicals listed in the ZDB available for interlibrary lending, these holdings are clearly designated. Approximately 95% of all titles recorded in the ZDB are held by the approximately 400 libraries participating in the interlibrary loan system.

The Internet has already paved the way into the future and the ZDB is working on developing further innovative services, such as the implementation of an online ordering component and link-ups to periodicals contents databases. *Die Deutsche Bibliothek*, which up until now has catalogued periodicals published in Germany independently from the ZDB, will in future contribute to the periodicals database. Additional plans are being made for the incorporation of periodicals published in Germany, or in the German language, held by foreign libraries. The ZDB has also begun recording electronic periodicals, cooperating for this purpose with the Electronic Periodicals Library (*Elektronische Zeitschriften-Bibliothek – EZB*) maintained by the University of Regensburg.

Bibliographies of Early Imprints

Since Germany had to exist well into the 20th century without a national library, it follows that there was also no national bibliography to document printed materials published in Germany since the invention of the movable letter-press. At no time was there talk of compiling a retrospective bibliography, but various catalog projects of supra-regional importance compiled from holdings reported by selected libraries and limited to the works of particular centuries can be regarded as an acceptable substitute.

The State Library in Berlin is still working on the compilation of the Union Catalog of Incunabula begun in 1904, the only complete bibliography of incunabula and fulfilling a catalog function as well, thanks to the information it contains on copies held by libraries all over the world. The Bavarian State Library houses the German section of the *Incunabula Short Title Catalogue* (ISTC), an international incunabula database edited by the British Library in London. A database containing the incunabula holdings in German collections is available on CD-ROM and includes digital illustrations of key pages.

The task of recording the bibliographical details of all printed materials published in the centuries following the incunabula era is dependent on co-operative effort. The "Index of Printed Materials Published in German-Speaking Countries in the 16th Century" (*Verzeichnis der im deutschen Sprachbereich erschienenen Drucke des XVI. Jahrhunderts*, VD 16), a bibliography published by the Bavarian State Library in collaboration with the Herzog August Library in Wolfenbüttel, was begun in 1983 and has since been completed. It contains about 80,000 entries, including the holdings of other libraries and a number of bibliographies. In a second phase, the holdings of around 30 German libraries not included in the published bibliography were compiled to form a supplement containing at present around 25,000 further titles, held as a database. To complete the 22 volumes of the printed edition, an electronic location database is being developed, containing information on libraries holding identical copies of the listed works.

A similar project, VD 17, scheduled for completion in ten to twelve years, was commenced in 1996 with the participation of nine large academic libraries, and like VD 16 is funded by the DFG. The objective of VD 17 is to catalog all works printed and published in the historical German-speaking region, regardless of the language of publication. Each work will be inspected prior to being catalogued according to RAK, and the bibliographic description will be enhanced with special characteristics which have been developed to aid the identification of older materials in a manner similar to a fingerprint. In addition, the key pages (title page, commencement of the main text, colophon, etc.) will be filmed and the microfilm then digitalized. The VD 17 database with its versatile search function will fulfill all the criteria required of a bibliography of older materials and is a further step along the road to a chronological German national bibliography.

The *Handbook of Historical Book Collections in Germany*

The *Handbook of Historical Book Collections in Germany* (*Handbuch der historischen Buchbestände*), published in 27 volumes by the Georg Olms Publishing House, can be regarded as a supplement to the retrospective national bibliography and like the latter, it is a cooperative venture launched by German libraries as well. In contrast to conventional catalogues and bibliographies, the *Handbook* concentrates not on individual works but on library collections in their entirety. It is conceived as an inventory of works published from the beginnings of the book printing era until the end of the 19th century and includes all literary genres, drawing no distinction between German and foreign publications. It provides a chronological and systematic outline of the historical collections of around 1,500 German libraries of all varieties, its classification by Federal *Länder* reflecting the regional character of the German library system.

The *Handbook of Historical Book Collections in Germany* represents a new form of working aid for academic and library work and is particularly directed at those research disciplines with a historical bias. Coverage has been extended to neighboring countries: The *Handbook of Historical Book Collections in Austria (Handbuch der historischen Buchbestände in Österreich)*, published in four volumes, describes the holdings of more than 250 libraries, while the *Handbook of German Historical Book Collections in Europe (Handbuch deutscher historischer Buchbestände in Europa)* surveys the collections of selected libraries with especially extensive and significant holdings. The *Handbook's* three sections combine to form a record of European cultural history.

User Services Cooperation

An excellent example of German library cooperation in the field of user services is the interlibrary lending system (*Fernleihe*, sometimes also called the *Überregionaler* or *Deutscher Leihverkehr*). The system's roots go back to the 19th century, and today interlibrary loan facilities are provided as a standard service, though struggling against modern document ordering and delivery systems which are better able to bridge the gap between rapid retrieval and slow delivery.

The Herzogin Anna Amalia Library in Weimar has its namesake Duchess (who was elected library patroness in 1991) to thank for its particularly magnificent rococo library hall, completed in 1766. In 2001 work was begun on an extension to the building and the subsequent renovation of the historical library tract is expected to be completed by 2006. The library is an active contributor to various projects for cataloging older materials and publishes a bibliography of German literature from the Classical Period.

Supraregional Interlibrary Loan and Electronic Document Delivery Services

No library has ever been able to provide every book, periodical and information source its users may require, and this is no less true today than in the past. It was for this reason that the interlending system was developed at the beginning of the 20th century as a form of reciprocal assistance. Today the supraregional interlibrary loan system is organized on a national basis and is directed exclusively at teaching and research. In addition, it supplies academic literature for training and occupational purposes.

Following the Second World War, regional catalogs were established both as a way of finding out what holdings German libraries actually had and as a basis for an interlibrary loan system. Some of these central catalogs covered single Federal *Länder*, others were more broadly-based. They were usually attached to large, regionally active li-

The library of the former Benedictine monastery at Amorbach (*Benediktinerabtei Amorbach*) in Franconia (Bavaria), privately owned by the Princes of Leiningen since secularization in 1803, is a masterpiece of early Classicism, housed in the convent building (1789 – 1799). Plain white dominates the décor of the room, including the bookshelves and finely carved staircases. The collection of 31,000 volumes, to which additions today are seldom made, is indexed in the *Handbook of Historical Book Collections in Germany*.

The Württemberg State Library (*Württembergische Landesbibliothek)* in Stuttgart was home to the central catalog until the foundation of the Baden-Württemberg Library Service Center (*Bibliotheksservicezentrum Baden-Württemberg*). Founded in 1765, the library owns outstanding collections of special and older material, including a famous Bible collection, and maintains its own research center, the Hölderlin Archives, which publishes the *Internationale Hölderlin-Bibliographie*. Incorporated into the Library is the Library of Contemporary History (*Bibliothek für Zeitgeschichte*), a special library focusing on contemporary history and war history since the First World War.

braries and many have been transferred to the regional union catalogs. There are at present ten central catalogs in Germany, assigned to the ten interlibrary loan regions; they are based in Berlin, Frankfurt am Main, Dresden, Göttingen, Halle, Hamburg, Cologne, Jena, Munich and Stuttgart.

Interlibrary lending was formerly mainly regionally based and here the central catalogs played an indispensable role in title location within their own areas. By the beginning of the 1990s, the seven central regions of the pre-unification Federal Republic had more than 50 million titles on record. Today, the sole function of the central catalogs is the location of older holdings for which machine-readable records are not yet available. The network databases, and more recently search engines such as the KVK, have taken over supporting the interlibrary loan system.

The number of annual interlibrary loan requests doubled between 1966 and 1978 from one to two million. In 1995 more than three million interlibrary loan requests were processed. The number of participating libraries has also increased; there are at present more than 900 libraries registered in the supraregional interlibrary lending system. Their names and location codes (IDs) are listed in a location code index (*Sigel-Verzeichnis*), published by the State Library in Berlin, which is also responsible for allocating the codes.

Interlibrary lending does not operate solely on the supraregional level; as a rule, community library systems themselves organize internal interlibrary loan systems between the central library and the individual branch and mobile libraries. Some Federal *Länder* have developed a regional interlending structure connecting to the national system. Finally, there is the international interlending system in which German libraries also take part, with the State Library in Berlin acting as the German international ILL clearinghouse.

Traditional interlibrary loan is increasingly being replaced by new forms of direct document delivery, the main objective of which is to shorten delivery times. Using modern information and communications technology, direct document delivery enables the library to deal directly with the user instead of having to pass his or her request on to another library. This assumes that the user has access to the appropriate literature databases, but since nearly all libraries and library networks make their databases available on the Internet as online catalogs, this is usually the case. The past ten years have seen the establishment of a number of commercial document delivery services.

The German National Library of Medicine (*Deutsche Zentralbibliothek für Medizin*) provides a variety of ordering and delivery facilities for articles from its 18,000 biomedical journals. The Technical Information Library (*Technische Informationsbibliothek – TIB*) in Hanover supplies articles, books, reports and microforms to any address via the *TIBORDER-Online* system. It also provides online access to electronic journal articles. The German Central Library of Economics in Kiel (*Deutsche Zentralbibliothek für Wirtschaftswissenschaften*) maintains a document delivery service for both books and articles which can be accessed by users in Germany and abroad.

Many university libraries offer a Special Subject Collection Area Rapid Delivery Service (*Sondersammelgebiets-Schnelllieferdienst*) for their DFG-allocated subject areas. Article copies, and in some cases books, too, are sent directly to the user, both within and outside Germany. The library network centers have developed similar supraregional ordering systems with additional features such as indexes of all currently available digitalized documents and electronic full-text publications, periodicals contents indexes and the linking of CD-ROM databases to document delivery systems. The widespread acceptance of this new form of "interlending" is reflected in the statistics: for example, the online ordering system *GBVdirekt* receives approximately 700,000 requests per year. Another example is *JASON*, a commercial express service for journal articles, which are sent to the user's home or workplace by post, fax or e-mail.

SUBITO was founded in 1994 as a joint Federal (*Bund*) and state (*Länder*) initiative to speed up and improve literature and information delivery services (*Bund-Länder-Initiative zur Beschleunigung der Literatur- und Informationsdienste*). Today it has become one of the most important supraregional document delivery services. It defines itself as a customer-centered service enterprise operating on a market-oriented and internationally competitive basis. The partners of the SUBITO Working Group (*SUBITO-Arbeitsgemeinschaft*) or members of *SUBITO – Dokumente aus Bibliotheken, e.V.* (= SUBITO – Documents from Libraries, Inc.), which at the end of 2002/beginning of 2003 achieved the status of an incorporated society, currently include 28 efficient and productive universal and special libraries. The headquarters and full-time office is based in Berlin.

The document delivery service offers online search and ordering facilities, using the Internet to supply subject literature directly to the user's desk. Functions include not only the sending of articles copies but also of books, collections, dissertations and other returnable literature. Orders are processed electronically and article copies can be delivered online, by fax or by post. Delivery is either within three working days (normal service) or within twenty-four hours (express service), excluding Saturdays in both cases.

The University Library in Hanover and the Technical Information Library (*Technische Informationsbibliothek – TIB*) in Lower Saxony have experienced continual growth in the past decade. The new building erected in 1965 was expanded in 1986 and again in 1991; in 2002 another location was added. Present user facilities include eight subject reading rooms with a total of 400 seats. The TIB is funded jointly by the Federal government (*Bund*) and the regional states (*Länder*), but also raises an increasingly large amount of money itself through the sale of its services such as SUBITO.

Dokumente aus Bibliotheken e.V.

Prices are calculated according to the form and speed of delivery, and the user's category. There are separate categories for school pupils, students, commercial users, and private persons. The *SUBITO Library Service* is aimed at libraries in Germany and abroad, and enables its customers to offer their users a 72-hour delivery service for journal articles at a special price. The volume of orders placed with *SUBITO* has continually increased over the past years, reaching 735,00 in 2001. Together with the other document delivery systems, *SUBITO* has made a significant contribution to the improvement of literature provision in Germany, supplementing the traditional interlibrary loan system. It is as yet impossible to say how the restructuring of the "delivery landscape" in Germany and Europe will develop.

6   A Vision of the Library in 2015

The Future of Libraries and Information

Visions for 2007 and 2015

As tempting as the hypothetical reflections may be, it can only be speculation if one were to draft a *vision for the future* for the year 2015 which portrays how the German libraries of the future will look.

It would also be inappropriate to assume – on the basis of today's knowledge and the current situation – that one could draft a *single* scenario for the future that would even come close to depicting the possible realities of the year 2015. The ideas and expectations of those persons who forecast the future are too divergent from one another. Inevitably, though, we cannot avoid wanting to develop multiple models of a possible future – but which of those visions conceived of today will correspond to the later reality remains to be seen.

One of the most promising projects related to this idea started in the summer of 2002, after the *Bundesvereinigung Deutscher Bibliotheksverbände* (BDB) and the Bertelsmann Foundation had agreed to conduct a three-part study on the topic "Library 2007 – Library Development in Germany" (*Bibliothek 2007 – Bibliotheksentwicklung in Deutschland*).

On the basis of a comprehensive analysis of the current state of German librarianship begun in phase one, a future scenario is being developed in the second phase during 2003 with the assistance of groups of experts and professional ad hoc task forces. The interests of numerous information and library service vendors are also to be taken into consideration, as are the overall political, legal, and financial conditions which differ due to the federative governing system and the cultural autonomy of the communities. The idea of the project is structured in such a way that the complex tasks are divided into several subordinate areas. The goal of the second phase, "to present a national strategy paper for library development in Germany based on a model of how it should be," will be completed by the end of 2003. In phase three, in which the actual implementation and conversion of the model

Digital media, storage and networks will characterize the information and communications world in the future much more than they do today. Opened in 1997, the media library in the Communications and Media Center – KOMED of the Cologne Media Park (*Kommunikations- und Medienzentrum KOMED im Kölner Mediapark*) (North Rhine-Westphalia), belongs to the City Library of Cologne (*Stadtbibliothek Köln*) and is already prepared for the growing need for multimedia in the future. More than 15,000 audiovisual and digital media are held in open access areas totalling 750 sqm. Continuing education events, training sessions, and projects on the acquisition of media competencies round out the offerings of this institution.

or models should be completed by the year 2007, it will be the final task of the project partners to determine new strategies and methods and to carry out the concrete implementation of the theoretical model.

As unfocused as the library of the year 2007 from today's viewpoint may be – (at least this relatively near future image is already being worked on today) – the image of the not-so-distant decade point 2015 appears even more nebulous. Nevertheless, some statements and opinions will be collected and given below.

The authors of this book conducted a small survey of several professional and key figures of library and cultural prominence about their vision of the library of the future: *What image of the library do you think is most probable more than ten years from now? What tasks will libraries fulfill in the year 2015, which responsibilities and services will they need to fulfil, and what content offerings will they have to provide?*

From the answers – supplemented by a glance at the professional literature – a mosaic-like picture can be developed that could come close to the reality of tomorrow. However, there are also completely different prognoses. They can be found in the headlines, for instance, in April 2002 in the *Frankfurter Allgemeine Zeitung (FAZ)* where one could read: "Bury the Libraries!" It is not the development of "hybrid libraries," nor the parallel administration of print and electronic information, that the author of this article defines as the cultural mission of libraries, but rather the complete digitization of all information.

It is above all the information scientists who believe that libraries will only have a future when they converge with computer centers and multimedia centers to create a new infrastructure for information and communication. As the task of this newly created institution, the same information scientists see knowledge management, thus, the coordination of virtually all sources of knowledge completely represented in digital form. An archive of printed collections could certainly continue to exist, but with advancing digitization it would lose its meaning and deteriorate to a "book museum."

The following cited assessments do not share these more pessimistic views. But they originate primarily from librarians, publishers and writers – that is, from people who have a special relationship to the medium form *book*. In these answers, the belief is also reflected that one can participate in forming the future of libraries through active intervention and even steer it in certain directions. Most assuredly, attitudes of waiting for something to happen and passive observation are not adequate for modern times, but rather the active and creative participation in the process of forming the future is necessary. There is no lack of ideas or conceptions in Germany, but rather a deficit in the concrete realization of the concepts already available.

First of all, we pose several introductory hypotheses as the *expected contextual conditions*:

1. Thesis: *Education* as such will be the primary issue in the advancing 21st century. Education will influence the entire society – above all in the commercial and economic areas.
2. Thesis: The acquisition of information will not be the problem in the coming century, but rather *concentration on the most fundamental* and on the correct information: Quality instead of quantity will be the focus more than ever before.
3. Thesis: The *Marketplace "Library,"* which allows people to actually meet, must be designed completely differently than the isolated, lonely work place in front of the computer screen with its view into the "global village" of the Internet.
4. Thesis: The Library of 2015 must be available as a *space attached to a specific physical building* and as an independent part of the cultural life of a community integrated into the social life of that community: without a library building, a city would be without a soul, and its citizens could not find a true foothold in the virtual structure of globally networked machines.
5. Thesis: The relationship of the *print medium and the digitally stored medium* will come to rest at 50:50 by the end of 2015; the non-book proportion will then rise only insignificantly in the following decades.

The Survey of 2002

Concerning the question: **"How will the library of the year 2015 look? Will it still have a building or will it only exist virtually or digitally?"** – there was almost complete unanimity among those surveyed that libraries would still have a building, a "wrapping" and a physical form – even if more so-called *virtual libraries as a network of library databases* would evolve and continue to be optimized.

Author and journalist *Dieter E. Zimmer* comments on this: "*The* one library will not be found in 2015 just as it does not exist today. There are only different kinds of libraries in the plural. They have buildings, most of them will have the same buildings they have today, because there will not be enough money for new buildings. Functionally, they will be further developed. There will be more use of digital materials of all kinds."

Prof. Dr. *Peter Vodosek* (*Hochschule der Medien*, Stuttgart) added: "In 2015, there will still be library buildings as communication centers, learning sites and meeting points ('face-to-face function'). They will have changed their appearance, as they have always done up to today, not the least in the expansion of their spectrum of content and service offerings. Despite their new buildings, many libraries are still not comfortable places today, places to work, to learn, and to experience."

Prof. Dr. *Bernd Meyer* (*Deutscher Städtetag*, Cologne) sees the problem similarly: "The library of 2015 will and must have a building, if possible, centrally and prominently located, since it must be a place where people not only call up information (search for information), but also a public, cultural focal point, not just a (material) gateway (even if virtual) to the world, but also a place where people can meet with others and with cultural experiences."

Publisher and journalist Prof. Dr. *Klaus G. Saur* is more concrete: "The library of the year 2015 will still be housed in a building with unendingly many online work spaces and with a digital data center, which can perform information transfer worldwide, identifying and conveying information, placing orders for the region or for the university centrally, organizing payment and optimizing information access for all. The building will – in addition to that – still be needed for storing historical book collections which must continue to be accessible, as well as for the sale, for the storage, and for the circulation of unending numbers of textbooks and books for general reading which cannot be substituted by any information technology." Ironically he added: "A small special department for *Festschriften* will be available which will also only be possible in finely printed form and will continue to be published unhindered."

Dr. *Herman Leskien* (General Director of the Bavarian State Library, Munich) believes, "that libraries will still be present which will not only provide external services, but also – most certainly – specialized knowledge about subject-oriented professional information. It is solely because of these components, which are based on the understanding that information is better communicated in person-to-person relationships than in the machine-to-person combination, thus there is little likelihood of libraries existing without buildings. However, it cannot be completely ruled out as there are anonymous professional agencies and banks without offices. Users of this type of library will not have the desire to look inside a book or to borrow it, they are looking for advice and training."

Neue Büchereibauten in Bayern

"Bibliotheken für heute und morgen" (Libraries for today and tomorrow): Since 1990, more than 100 public and academic libraries have been built in Germany, whereby the distribution between the Western and the Eastern German states is about equal. Modern public libraries with remarkable buildings emerged especially in the central cities of the South and Southeast parts of Germany. The architecture of several of these new buildings, for instance in *Deggendorf* (Bavaria), gives an impression as to how the library of tomorrow could look.

In answer to the question **"What will the future offering of media look like?"** most of the persons queried are convinced that the variety of digital storage mediums will experience one or two new developments, but in essence, the spectrum of offerings will look exactly as it does in the year 2003. The major medium for libraries – everyone agrees on this – still remains the printed book.

"Non-book media will be made accessible online in extraordinary large numbers in the year 2015," says *Klaus G. Saur*. "In addition, there will still be historically relevant microfiches and microfilm editions, as well as security filming of one's own collections and further materials which – whether due to technical aspects or due to cost aspects – are not suitable for digitizing, but must be kept. Books will still be present."

"Wherever literature is art," *Hannelore Jouly* (former director of the City Library of Stuttgart) believes, "the book will have significance for a long time. I wish that the book would evolve more into a form of art. In certain areas, books will also remain practical for learning and as a compendium of knowledge. Books retain a central value – even when the number of books decreases. As a storage medium for information and current discussion, books will be replaced to a great degree by electronic media which also produces great advantages: currency, linking possibilities, interactivity, etc."

Dr. *Elisabeth Niggemann* (General Director of *Die Deutsche Bibliothek*, Frankfurt/Main) goes a step farther with her vision of media: "For *Die Deutsche Bibliothek* as 'memory of the nation' all conventional and digital media will still play a role in the year 2015, because in our mission we will still maintain all types of media permanently, that is, for eternity, collecting, archiving, indexing, cataloguing, and making them available. Surely, the electronic media will have matured and will have attained a secure place in the information chain. But in addition, a forced further development of conventional media could also take place, for instance, 'comfortable books,' which one could fall asleep upon, or books in which one could browse and page through and which read themselves aloud, or travel books which provide the smells and sounds of the areas being described ..."

Hermann Leskien is convinced of the variety of media, but he considers some of the media as being temporary and thus limited. "It can be seen that in the field of information carriers and of media design a great variety could evolve. There will often be – as was the case with the CD-ROM – transitional phenomena. In any case, books, newspapers, journals will be available, but also networked publications, online newspapers, and e-journals, just to mention a few of the text-bound media. Probably, multimedia, despite all of the current propaganda and promotional advertising, will achieve only a limited place value. The reasons for this lie in the fact that personnel effort and costs are very high, and this is only worthwhile if large amounts of money can be invested. Thus, the breadth of material is very narrow, because it nec-

The new building of the Thuringian University and State Library (*Thüringer Universitäts- und Landes-bibliothek) in Jena* (Architects: Heckmann, Kristel, Jung), opened in 2001, may give an answer to the question as to whether libraries in the age of data networks will still need a building. The single-level library system of Jena, which makes 3,9 million media units available, consists of the central library and almost 30 branch and partial libraries in the city area – which are to be decreased in several steps.

essarily concerns popular themes with a relatively long half-life."

If one poses the question on the "Production and distribution of publications and information in the year 2015 and the future actors and producers," then the answers and the expected trends are not so divergent.

Graham Jefcoate (The British Library, London) is of the opinion that serious changes compared to the present system are hardly probable: "The landscape will possibly *not* have a fundamentally different appearance than it does today. The 'freeing-up' of the market through networks placed into question by the publishers may not take place as some today believe or wish [that it would]."

Even the writer and essayist Prof. Dr. *Peter Härtling* is convinced: "Book stores, publishers, probably even book warehouses and Internet dealers will prevail."

Dieter E. Zimmer is of the opinion that "professional mediating agencies which cannot exactly be called 'publishers' in the area of digital media, but will rather grow out of an English designation" will be the determining actors in the media market.

Dieter Schormann (Chairman of the Association of the German Book Trade) sees the parallel existence of different producers: "Even here there will be a virtual and a digital neighborhood in 2015. Everyone will be able to publish – whether it be in the 'books on demand' process or on the Internet. However, we need filters, that is, a completely new type of editorial department, and sponsors for authors."

Peter Vodosek believes: "In addition to traditional production and distribution, publishing on demand will play a greater role – even up to a specific degree direct individual self-publishing in the network. Document delivery services on a private commercial basis will increase. Libraries will retain their function as a neutral provider of selected information based on qualitative aspects."

Elisabeth Niggemann expresses her opinion even more concretely: "Through PC's with increasingly cheaper price tags and higher performance levels, reduced Internet fees, and electronic publishing procedures, anyone can become author and publisher on his own. The traditional publication chain author-publisher-reader will surely have to be rethought, but it will not disappear. Virtual information mediators will still be present to assist the information seeker. The competent evaluation and selection of content will be 'necessary for survival' in the increasingly threatening flood of useful and useless information. In that process, the producers and distributors of knowledge could increasingly become moderators and all-round providers. This will be especially clear with electronic publications. In addition to the access to information and publications, chat rooms and discussion lists can be visited, the reader/user can be linked from his selected item to related topics and publications, and he can inform himself regularly via mail on current developments."

Hermann Leskien believes several changes will take place – all the way up to a role change and growth in importance of research institutions – when he notes: "Production and distribution of publications in 2015 will no longer be determined by an inflexible role system. That does not mean that the publishers have to give up their dominant position. But there will be a greater variety of equally valued paths, differing from subject to subject and from country to country. The major requirement is the quality assurance of the niveau. In that respect, only the authors are excluded as independent producers of relevant literature, probably also the libraries, at least in Germany. On the other hand, learned societies, institutions (such as universities and research institutions), as well as institutional associations, will take on a new significance as producers and distributors. Among all the actors an intensive cooperation will develop in any case so that not only competition, but also new formation of networks will play a role."

It is interesting to see **"which specific subject descriptors, functions and tasks for the library of the year 2015"** came to mind for those experts surveyed. In their vision, the interview partners proceeded from the premise that the future library can be described with the following terms regarding its "primary functions" listed here in order of the frequency of occurrence:

(1) Media Center / Information Center, (2) Document Center, (3) Data Center, (4) Lending Library, (5) Call Center, (6) Cultural Center, (7) Computer Center, (8) Full Text Server, (9) Place of Learning,

Whether the digital media will truly suppress printed works is still doubted by many of the experts. Instead, it is expected that the number of books and non-books will equalize and exist parallel to one another whereas the production costs, marketing costs, and presentation forms will definitely differ from today. In the *Konrad Duden City Library of Bad Hersfeld (Hesse)*, newly opened in 1999, customers can work, surf, and chat at 12 combined OPAC- and Internet computers mostly in the form of PC carrels.

(10) Long-term Archive, (11) Internet Café, (12) Book Museum, (13) Citizens' Information Office.

Two variations can be extracted from the answers, when careful interpretation is used:

Model 1: More than 75% of those questioned see the library of the future predominately as a mixture of *Media Center* and *Information Center*, *Call Center* and *Citizens' Information Office* connected with the additional roles of a *Place of Learning* and a *Book Museum*. However, it is conspicuous that the museum aspects, the aspects of book history, and the archival aspects are named as important aspects of the library of the future more often than not.

Model 2: More than 50% of those questioned saw the library of the future as a predominant mixture of a *Document Center* and *Full Text Server*, whereby the role as a *Cultural Center* is integrated with that of an *Internet Café*.

The greatest reservation and scepticism was expressed regarding the idea of convergence where the library of the future would tend in the direction of a *Computer Center* which would function alone as a *Central Data Center* possibly with an *Internet Café* attached to it and still retain museum-oriented book collections in a special department. Even the thought that the library of tomorrow would be transformed solely into a *Citizens' Information Office* was rejected by most of those interviewed.

If we assume that services and tasks of the library will change, it is important to ask **"Which new areas of activity should libraries definitely take on and develop in the future?"**

Peter Vodosek remarks: "We do not live in an information society (informed society), but rather in a society with a vast offering of information. Information only leads to quality when users learn how to use it. The consequence of this: More literary promotion, more continuing education ('learning studios,' 'teaching library,' etc.). Future new-old fields will exist: Improvement of service; however, making new tools available is no substitution for service."

Elisabeth Niggemann suspects the same, when she writes: "The library of the future will (which is not new) have to be more engaged in reading promotion and cultivation of media competencies than before."

Klaus G. Saur is of the opinion: "The library or rather the information center of the future must be

Maybe even more intensely than today, people in the future will make sure that their library has an aesthetically pleasing architecture and that it offers them an atmosphere for relaxation and communication which can be sensually experienced via the library's function as a storage place of knowledge. The Public Library of the community of Neufahrn, Bavaria (*Gemeindebücherei Neufahrn*), constructed in the form of a ship with a „Bug" made of glass, differing window forms, and a staircase bathed in light could lead the way into modern library architecture.

much more fundamentally oriented to data processing technology and also provide more comprehensive advisory services in order to guarantee the optimal level of information opportunities. It must become possible to offer as comprehensively as possible complete information packages and texts that are freely available or moderately priced, and references to texts which, if not directly available, can be obtained."

Dieter E. Zimmer is convinced: "Above all: online indexing of complete collections (retroconversion), integrating catalog data into regional union catalogs, expanding the digital cataloguing of collections to small and drowsy libraries. Full text digitization of large reference works and at least one daily newspaper for the entire 20th century."

An image which is familiar to us comes from *Hannelore Jouly*: "Possibly the public library will become a campus in the future in which networks of educational and cultural institutions will work together to create a public space as an atmosphere for innovation. The focal point will be learning,

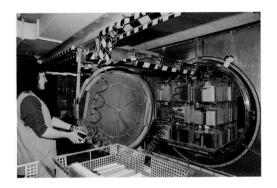

According to estimates, of the approximately 135 million books published in Germany after 1840 about 12% are already disintegrated and are thus no longer able to be used; a further 30% are so deeply yellowed that to avoid further damage they should actually be taken out of use. Only in special cases can restoration of individual books be carried out in order to save these books; alternatively a massive deacidification could be considered, such as carried out in the Center for Book Preservation (*Zentrum für Bucherhaltung GmbH*) in Leipzig (Saxony).

concentration, debate, information, advice, participation, genuine experience ..."

Hermann Leskien is skeptical as to whether the tasks of the library will change fundamentally and new ones will be added, because "Knowledge and knowledge transfer have functionally and fundamentally run in similar tracks for a very long time. But the efforts which are being demanded from libraries will be so immense that it will have the appearance of dealing with a new level of quality. Thus libraries (together with archives) will have to take on, for instance, the long-term archiving of publications. What was previously most likely taken care of by placing the book onto the shelf will constantly demand a supreme effort with respect to the technological development and must guarantee that the information content can always be migrated into the current state of the art technology. This will only be able to be carried out in very few institutions to which others will have to turn and depend upon within a network. Similarly, cataloging and indexing will certainly no longer be a prod-

uct of individual achievement in the future; rather it must result from a secondary harmonization in the sense of a customer-orientation – actually not a new task, but a fully new aspect of an age-old function of libraries."

Prof. *Birgit Dankert* (former Speaker of the BDB) sees the future of libraries very strongly in context of the motto "Local Access, Global Information", when, as a facet of her future vision, she notes: "Libraries have to succeed – academic and research libraries, as well as pubic libraries – in driving the digitization of media, media transmission, information activities, and structuring of knowledge, and thereby provide so-called models and give guidance and direction. At the same time, libraries must remain cultural institutions or some of them become cultural institutions, a first access point for information, for cultural evidence, for functions, for questions, for cultural events in the local surrounding areas. That the enterprising focus will take precedence more than was the case before, and that one must manage culture, should not be ignored.

The digitization centers in Munich (Bavaria) and Göttingen (Lower Saxony), financed by the DFG, support the development of the Distributed Digital Research Library (*Verteilte Digitale Forschungsbibliothek*) by making digital resources available and presenting them. The *Munich Digitalization Center (Münchener Digitalisierungszentrum* – MDZ) at the Bavarian State Library (picture right) carries out its own projects, but also takes on digitization projects from other institutions on commission. Nine Special Subject Area Libraries under the leadership of the Göttingen Library (*Staats- und Universitätsbibliothek Göttingen*) have formed a consortium for the digitization of journal collections.

GUTENBERG
DIGITAL

The Göttingen Digitalization Center (*Göttinger Digitalisierungszentrum (GDZ)*) used the 600th birthday of Johannes Gutenberg as the occasion to scan all 1282 pages of the parchment copy of the *Gutenberg Bible* belonging to the State and University Library of Lower Saxony (*Staats- und Universitätsbibliothek Göttingen* (Niedersachsen)) and offer it both on the Internet and as a CD-ROM edition. Between the first printing which Gutenberg produced with the help of new technology, and the digitalization in the year 2000 of precisely this first print edition was a span of approximately 550 years of book and library history.

And if one thinks about it, the thing that would be damaging on the way to this vision of electronic data transfer and the library as a cultural institutions is the disappearance of infrastructures which have taken a long, hard road to build up in publishing and the book trade, in libraries and library associations. What cannot happen in any case is that the libraries in their future development engage in some sort of media competition – that is, one media form will be played out against another – or that they let themselves be driven into the larger marketing strategies and commercialization of media. They must retain their independence and a position which allows them to deal with the products of global media producers according to the libraries' goals."

Dieter Schormann summarizes his viewpoint in the form of an admonition: "In the future, libraries must provide direction and more orientation for, as well as lead and motivate the users. The library of the future will have to take an important place in the cultural considerations made in the communities. Without the library, there will be no future."

Epilogue

Ten years after the publication of the standard work *Bibliotheken '93. Strukturen, Aufgaben, Positionen* (*Libraries '93. Structures, Tasks, Positions*), the Federation of German Library Associations (*Bundesvereinigung Deutscher Bibliotheksverbände – BDB*) presents a comprehensive summary and overview of librarianship in Germany in the "Portals to the Past and to the Future." Of course, the character of the this present book differs totally from the work published ten years ago; this is already reflected in its external design.

The authors, Jürgen Seefeldt and Dr. Ludger Syré, were given the task of writing an easily readable text on German librarianship – which they also wanted to do – as well as designing a richly illustrated overview. In context of the IFLA Conference taking place in Berlin 2003, our intention was to offer an overall portrayal of German librarianship which would also give non-German, interested persons not a complete, but a relatively comprehensive glimpse into the German library landscape. With that, we want to emphasize what this book is not: it is not a handbook which comprehensively lists all Germany library situations in detail. Instead, this book describes the main characteristics and sets accents; certain libraries and projects are listed as exemplary for the rest; numerous pictures are intended to demonstrate the variety of German librarianship. To write in this brevity and to select the pictures was as difficult task, for which the *Bundesvereinigung Deutscher Bibliotheksverbände* congratulates and thanks the two authors for their success in achieving this. It is also difficult to translate the very complex and socio-professionally embedded text into a foreign language; we thus thank Dr. Diann Rusch-Feja for her English translation and Janet MacKenzie for her assistance with Chapter Five.

The financial basis for producing this book was made possible by the Berlin Senate and above all the *Goethe Institute Inter Nationes (GIIN)*. We also thank the GIIN, specifically by name, Susanne Höhn, Christel Mahnke and Christiane Bohrer, for various means of support of our international work which has had to be organized completely on a voluntary basis. The fact that this work has been successful both qualitatively and quantitatively, is due to the commitment and work of the task force "Library & Information International" (*Bibliothek & Information International*) of the BDB with its chairwoman, Ulrike Lang, and to the availability of project funding through the "Cultural Foundation of the *Länder*" (*Kulturstiftung der Länder*).

The good fairy of IFLA 2003 was and is our lady in Berlin, Barbara Schleihagen. She and her co-workers, Christoph Albers and Irina Courzakis, have contributed valuably to the IFLA in building up our international contacts during the past years in an extraordinary manner and thereby also building up the image of German librarianship abroad. To them and to the members of the Working Group responsible for Publications within the *IFLA 2003 National Organization Committee* go our thanks for their support in preparing this publication. In addition, I thank all the institutions which have provided photographic materials for this publication.

If the level of commitment shown on the occasion of preparing for this IFLA Conference and in producing this publication is indicative of the work of our libraries and if it continues at this level, then despite all external and internal difficulties, I am not concerned about fulfilling our future information, cultural and educational commitments. Thus, German libraries can step through the portal to the future with courage, confidence, and satisfaction with their accomplishments.

Berlin, January 2003
Dr. Georg Ruppelt
Speaker of the *Bundesvereinigung Deutscher Bibliotheksverbände*

Appendices

Picture Reference

Picture Reference (in order of appearance in the text)

Alphabetical Index of Pictures by Location

Further Readings (A Selection)

Books

Bau- und Nutzungsplanung von wissenschaftlichen Bibliotheken /
Erarbeitet. im NA Bibliotheks- und Dokumentationswesen unter Mitwirkung einer Expertengruppe des Deutschen Bibliotheksinstituts (DBI). Hrsg.: DIN Deutsches Institut für Normung e.V. – 2. ed. – Berlin [et al.] : Beuth, 1998. – vi, 69 pp. – (DIN-Fachbericht ; 13). – ISBN 3-410-13831-5

Bibliothek des Jahres :
der nationale Bibliothekspreis der Jahre 2000, 2001 und 2002 / Hrsg.: Zeit-Stiftung Ebelin und Gerd Bucerius und Deutscher Bibliotheksverband e.V.. – Berlin : DBV, 2002. – 36 pp.

Bibliotheken '93 :
Strukturen, Aufgaben, Positionen / Bundesvereinigung Deutscher Bibliotheksverbände. – Berlin : Deutsches Bibliotheksinstitut ; Göttingen : Niedersächsische Staats- u. Univ.-Bibliothek, 1994. – vi, 182 pp. : Ill. – ISBN 3-87068-445-3 (DBI). – ISBN 3-930457-00-8 (NSuUB)

Bibliotheken im Zeitalter der Datenautobahnen und internationalen Netze /
[veröffentlicht im Rahmen des 85. Deutschen Bibliothekartages Göttingen 1995] / erarbeitet von der BDB Arbeitsgruppe Elektronische Medien in Bibliotheken. Andreas Anderhub ... – 2. ed. – Berlin, 1996. – 4 pp.

Bibliothekspolitik in Ost und West :
Geschichte und Gegenwart des Deutschen Bibliotheksverbandes / hrsg. von Georg Ruppelt. – Frankfurt am Main : Klostermann, 1998. – vi, 322 pp.; (Zeitschrift für Bibliothekswesen und Bibliographie : Sonderhefte ; 72). – ISBN 3-465-02999-2

Berufsbild 2000 – Bibliotheken und Bibliothekare im Wandel /
erarb. von der Arbeitsgruppe "Gemeinsames Berufsbild" der BDB e.V. Unter Leitung von Ute Krauß-Leichert. – 2., unveränd. Nachdr. der dt. Fassung, erg. um die engl. Version. – Wiesbaden : Dinges und Frick, 2000. – 125 pp. – ISBN 3-934997-01-5

Buzás, Ladislaus :
Deutsche Bibliotheksgeschichte des Mittelalters / Ladislaus Buzás. – Wiesbaden : Reichert, 1975. – 191 pp.; (Elemente des Buch- und Bibliothekswesens ; 1). – ISBN 3-920153-48-0, 3-920153-49-9

Buzás, Ladislaus :
Deutsche Bibliotheksgeschichte der Neuzeit (1500 – 1800) / Ladislaus Buzás. – Wiesbaden : Reichert, 1976. – 203 pp.; (Elemente des Buch- und Bibliothekswesens ; 2). – ISBN 3-920153-59-6, 3-920153-58-8

Buzás, Ladislaus :
Deutsche Bibliotheksgeschichte der neuesten Zeit (1800 – 1945) / Ladislaus Buzás. – Wiesbaden : Reichert, 1978. – 215 pp.; (Elemente des Buch- und Bibliothekswesens ; 3). – ISBN 3-920153-76-6, 3-920153-75-8

Entscheidungssammlung zum Bibliotheksrecht /
hrsg. von der Rechtskommission des Deutschen Bibliotheksinstituts ... Erarbeitet von: Jürgen Christoph Gödan ... – Berlin: Ehemaliges Dt. Bibliotheksinstitut, 2000. – 656 pp. – ISBN 3-87068-997-8

Erfolgreiches Management von Bibliotheken und Informationseinrichtungen :
Fachratgeber für die Bibliotheksleitung und Bibliothekare / Hrsg: Hans-Christoph Hobohm, Konrad Umlauf. – Hamburg: Dashöfer, 2002. – 700 pp. – ISBN 3-931832-46-5 – Loose leaf edition

Ewert, Gisela ; Umstätter, Walther :
Lehrbuch der Bibliotheksverwaltung / auf d. Grundlage d. Werkes von Wilhelm Krabbe u. Wilhelm Martin Luther völlig neu bearb. von Gisela Ewert u. Walther Umstätter. – Stuttgart : Hiersemann, 1997. – xv, 204 pp. – ISBN 3-7772-9730-5

Gaus, Wilhelm :
Berufe im Informationswesen : ein Wegweiser zur Ausbildung ; Archiv, Bibliothek, Buchwissenschaft, Information und Dokumentation, Medizinische Dokumentation, Medizinische Informatik, Computerlinguistik, Museum / Wilhelm Gaus. – 5., vollständig überarbeitete Aufl. – Berlin [u.a.] : Springer, 2002. – 310 pp. – ISBN 3-540-43619-7

Grundlagen der praktischen Information und Dokumentation :
ein Handbuch zur Einführung in die fachliche Informationsarbeit / Marianne Buder ... (Hrsg). Begr. von Klaus Laisiepen .... – 4., völlig neu gefasste Ausg. – Vols. 1.2. – Munich: Saur, 1997. – ISBN 3-598-11309-9, 3-598-21253-4

Gutachtensammlung zum Bibliotheksrecht :
Gutachten, Stellungnahmen, Empfehlungen, Berichte der Rechtskommission des Deutschen Bibliotheksinstituts und der Kommission für Rechtsfragen des Vereins Deutscher Bibliothekare / Deutsches Bibliotheksinstitut – Rechtskommission ; erarbeitet von einer Arbeitsgruppe der Rechtskommission des Ehemaligen Deutschen Bibliotheksinstituts (EDBI) und der Kommission für Rechtsfragen des Vereins Deutscher Bibliothekare (VDB) e.V.: Gabriele Beger ... Red.: Helmut Rösner. – Stand: Oktober 2001. – Wiesbaden: Harrassowitz, 2002. – xiv, 618 pp. (Bibliotheksrecht; Vol. 1). – ISBN 3-447-04541-8

Hacker, Rupert :
Bibliothekarisches Grundwissen. – 7., neubearb. Auflage. – Munich: Saur, 2000. – 366 pp. – ISBN 3-598-11394-3

Handbuch Lesen /
im Auftr. der Stiftung Lesen u. der Deutschen Literaturkonferenz hrsg. von Bodo Granzmann. – Baltmannsweiler: Schneider Verl. Hohengehren, 2001. – xi, 690 pp. – ISBN 3-89676-495-0

Handbuch der Bibliotheken Deutschland, Österreich, Schweiz.
– 8. Aufl. – Munich : Saur, 2002. – ISBN 3-598-11568-7

Jahrbuch der Deutschen Bibliotheken /
hrsg. vom Verein Deutscher Bibliothekare. – Wiesbaden : Harrassowitz
Vol. 59. (2001/02). – 2001.

Jahrbuch der Öffentlichen Bibliotheken /
hrsg. vom Berufsverband Bibliothek Information e.V. Bearb. von Petra Hauke. – Bad Honnef: Bock + Herchen, Ausg. 2000/01. – 2001. – 331 pp. – ISBN 3-88347-212-3

Jochum, Uwe :
Kleine Bibliotheksgeschichte / von Uwe Jochum. – 2., durchgesehene. und bibliographisch ergänzte Aufl.. – Stuttgart : Reclam, 1999. – 232 pp.; (Universal-Bibliothek ; No. 8915 : Reclam Wissen). – ISBN 3-15-008915-8

Krieg, Werner :
Einführung in die Bibliothekskunde. – 2. Aufl. / besorgt von Rudolf Jung. – Darmstadt : Wiss. Buchges., 1990. vi, 184 pp. – ISBN 3-534-08629-5

Plassmann, Engelbert; Seefeldt, Jürgen :
Das Bibliothekswesen der Bundesrepublik Deutschland : ein Handbuch / von Engelbert Plassmann und Jürgen Seefeldt. – 3., völlig

neubearbeitete Auflage des durch Gisela von Busse und Horst Ernestus begründeten Werkes. – Wiesbaden : Harrassowitz Verlag 1999, Wiesbaden. – xii, 510 pp., maps, illus. – ISBN 3-447-03706-7

Politik für Bibliotheken : die Bundesvereinigung Deutscher Bibliotheksverbände (BDB) im Gespräch ; Birgit Dankert zum Ende ihrer Amtszeit als Sprecherin der BDB / hrsg. von Georg Ruppelt. – Munich : Saur, 2000. – 208 pp. – ISBN 3-598-11436-2

Politik für öffentliche Bibliotheken/ Bundesvereinigung Deutscher Bibliotheksverbände ; Plattform Öffentliche Bibliotheken. Hrsg. von Konrad Umlauf. Mit Beitr. von Rolf-Peter Carl ... – Bad Honnef : Bock + Herchen, 1998. – 121 pp. – (Bibliothek und Gesellschaft). – ISBN 3-88347-199-2

Regionalbibliotheken in Deutschland: mit einem Ausblick auf Österreich und die Schweiz / hrsg. von Bernd Hagenau. – Frankfurt am Main : Klostermann, 2000. – 467 pp., 1 map; (Zeitschrift für Bibliothekswesen und Bibliographie : Sonderheft ; 78). – ISBN 3-465-03085-0

Röttcher, Günter ; Böttger, Klaus Peter ; Ankerstein, Ursula : Basiswissen Bibliothek : Fachkunde für Assistentinnen u. Assistenten an Bibliotheken ; die theoretischen u. praktischen Grundlagen e. Bibliotheksberufes / Günter Röttcher ; Klaus Peter Böttger ; Ursula Ankerstein. – 3., überarbeitete u. aktualisierte Aufl. – Bad Honnef : Bock + Herchen, 1995. – 343 pp.,: illus. – (Bibliothek und Gesellschaft). – ISBN 3-88347-177-1

Rothmann, Peter Heinz : Multimedia-Schulbibliothek – Leseförderung mit neuen Medien / Peter Heinz Rothmann. – Amberg: Buch- und Kunstverlag Oberpfalz, 2002. – 24 pp. – ISBN 3-935719-07-8

Seidel, Stefanie : Die schönsten Räume, die wertvollsten Sammlungen; Deutschland, Österreich, Schweiz. – Munich: Callwey, 1995. – 191 pp., Illus. – ISBN 3-7667-1156-3

Spezialbibliotheken in Deutschland / Red. Petra Hauke. Unter Mitarb. Von Gisela Bartz. – Bad Honnef: Bock + Herchen, 1996-2002. Vols. 1-5.

Umlauf, Konrad : Bestandsaufbau an öffentlichen Bibliotheken / Konrad Umlauf. – Frankfurt a.M. : Klostermann, 1997.

– 413 pp. – (Das Bibliothekswesen in Einzeldarstellungen). – ISBN 3-465-02926-7

Umlauf, Konrad : Medienkunde / Konrad Umlauf unter Mitarbeit von Daniella Sarnowski. – Wiesbaden : Harrassowitz, 2000. – 344 pp. – (Bibliotheksarbeit 8). – ISBN 3-447-04326-1

Umlauf, Konrad : Moderne Buchkunde / Konrad Umlauf. – Wiesbaden : Harrassowitz, 1996. – 191 pp. – (Bibliotheksarbeit ; 2). – ISBN 3-447-03870-5

Journals

ABI-Technik : Zeitschrift für Automation, Bau und Technik im Archiv-, Bibliotheks- und Informationswesen. / Hrsg.: Rudolf Frankenberger u.a. – Munich : Verlag Neuer Merkur. – *Published Quarterly.*

Auskunft : Zeitschrift für Bibliothek, Archiv und Information in Norddeutschland (hrsg. im Auftr. des Lnadesverbandes Hamburg im DBV von Petra Blödorn-Meyer u.a. – Staats- und Universitätsbibliothek Hamburg. – *Published Quarterly.*

Bibliothek : Forschung und Praxis / Hrsg.: Paul Kaegbein u.a. – Munich: Saur. – *Published every four months.*

Bibliotheksdienst / Redaktion, Herstellung und Vertrieb: Zentral und Landesbibliothek Berlin. – *Published monthly.*

Bibliotheksforum Bayern : BFB / Red.: Mathias Hänel. Bayerische Staatsbibliothek. – Munich : Saur. – *Published every four months.*

B.I.T.-Online : Zeitschrift für Bibliothek, Information und Technologie mit aktueller Internet-Präsenz / Hrsg.: Rolf Fuhlrott u.a. – Wiesbaden : Dinges & Frick. – *Published quarterly.*

BuB : Forum für Bibliothek und Information ; Fachzeitschrift des BIB e.V., Berufsverband Information Bibliothek / Hrsg.: Konrad Umlauf u.a. – Bad Honnef : Bock + Herchen. – *Published ten times a year.*

Die Bücherei – Zeitschrift für Öffentliche Bibliotheken in Rheinland-Pfalz / Hrsg.: Jürgen Seefeldt u.a. – Landesbüchereistelle Rheinland-Pfalz und Staatliche Büchereistelle Rheinhessen-Pfalz. – Coblence : Görres. – *Published semi-annually.*

Buchprofile für die katholische Büchereiarbeit / Hrsg.: Borromäusverein e.V. Bonn und St. Michaelsbund. – Bonn : BV. – *Published quarterly.*

Dialog mit Bibliotheken : Fachzeitschrift über Die Deutsche Bibliothek, ihre Aktivitäten, ihr Dienstleistungsangebot / Red.: Kristina Knull-Schlomann. – Frankfurt/Main : DDB. – *Published every four months.*

Der Evangelische Buchberater : Zeitschrift für Buch- und Büchereiarbeit / Hrsg.: Deutscher Verband Evangelischer Büchereien. – Göttingen : DVEB. – *Published quarterly.*

Information – Wissenschaft und Praxis : Nfd / Red.: Marlies Ockenfeld. Hrsg. von der Deutschen Gesellschaft für Informationswissenschaft und Informationspraxis. – .Wiesbaden : Dinges & Frick. –*Published quarterly.*

Die Katholische öffentliche Bücherei : KÖB ; Vierteljahresschrift für Mitarb. der katholischen öffentlichen Büchereien / Red.: Rolf Pitsch. Hrsg.: Borromäusverein. – Bonn : BV. – *Published quarterly.*

LIES – Lesen, Informieren, Erleben in der Schulbibliothek : Arbeitshilfen und Informationen für Schulbibliotheken ; eine Schriftenreihe für die zentralen Schulbibliotheken des Landes Rheinland-Pfalz / Hrsg. von der Kommission Zentrale Schulbibliotheken. – Wörth : Europa-Gymnasium. – *Published semi-annually.*

MB/GBV : Mitteilungsblatt der Bibliotheken in Niedersachsen und Sachsen-Anhalt und des Gemeinsamen Bibliotheksverbundes (GBV) / Hrsg.: Arbeitsgemeinschaft der Bibliotheken in Niedersachsen ; Arbeitsgemeinschaft der Bibliotheken in Sachsen-Anhalt. – Hanover : Niedersächsische Landesbibliothek. – *Published quarterly.*

ÖBiB : Öffentliche Bibliotheken in Bayern / Hrsg.: Bayerische Staatsbibliothek. – Munich : BSB. – *Published five times a year.*

ProLibris : Mitteilungsblatt / hrsg. vom Verband der Bibliotheken des Landes Nordrhein-Westfalen und den Bezirksregierungen. – Bonn : ULB. – *Published every four months.*

Zeitschrift für Bibliothekswesen und Bibliographie : vereinigt mit Zentralblatt für Bibliothekswesen ; ZfBB : Organ des wissenschaftlichen Bibliothekswesens / Hrsg.: Elisabeth Niggemann u.a. – Frankfurt/Main: Klostermann. – *Published every two months.*

Internet Addresses (A Selection)

Arbeitsgemeinschaft der Spezialbibliotheken
www.aspb.de

Bayerische Staatsbibliothek
www.bsb-muenchen.de

Bertelsmann Stiftung
www.bertelsmann-stiftung.de

Berufsverband Information Bibliothek
www.bib-info.de

Bibliothek & Information International
www.stbib-koeln.de/bi/bi-
international.html

Bibliothek 2007
www.bibliothek2007.de

Bibliotheksindex
www.bix-bibliotheksindex.de

Bibliotheksservice-Zentrum Baden
Württemberg
www.bsz-bw.de

Bibliotheksverbund Bayern
www.bib-bvb.de/

Büro der Europäischen Bibliotheksverbände
www.eblida.org.

Bundesvereinigung Deutscher Bibliotheksverbände
www.bdbverband.de

Die Deutsche Bibliothek
www.ddb.de

Deutsche Gesellschaft für Informationswissenschaft und Informationspraxis
www.dgi-info.de

Deutscher Bibliotheksverband
www.bibliotheksverband.de

Deutscher Bibliotheksverbund DBV-OSI
z3950gw.dbf.ddb.de/

Deutscher Bildungsserver
www.bildungsserver.de

Deutsche Bibliotheksstatistik
www.bibliotheksstatistik.de

Deutsche Internet-Bibliothek
www.internetbibliothek.de

Digitale Bibliothek Nordrhein-Westfalen
www.digibib.net

ekz-bibliotheksservice GmbH
www.ekz.de

EZB – Elektronische Zeitschriftenbiblio-
thek
www.bibliothek.uni-regensburg.de/
ezeit

Fachstellen-Server
www.fachstellen.de

Gemeinsamer Bibliotheksverbund
www.gbv.de

Goethe-Institut Inter Nationes
www.goethe.de

Hessisches
Bibliotheksinformationssystem
www.hebis.de

Hochschulbibliothekszentrum NRW
www.hbz-nrw.de

Internet-Informations- und -Lernzen-
trum Bibliothek
www.infolab-rlp.de

IFLA-Nationalkommitee Deutschland
www.ifla.deutschland.de

Karlsruher Virtueller Katalog
www.ubka.uni-karlsruhe.de/
kvk_alt.html

Kirchlicher Verbundkatalog
www.efh-hannover.de/bibliothek/
kivk/

Kooperativer Bibliotheksverbund Berlin-
Brandenburg
www.kobv.de

Staatsbibliothek zu Berlin PK
www.sbb.spk-berlin.de

SUBITO
www.subito-doc.de

Verein Deutscher Bibliothekare
www.vdb-online.org

Virtuelle Deutsche Landesbibliographie
www.ubka.uni-karlsruhe.de/
landesbibliographie/

Virtuelle Fachbibliotheken und
Informationsverbünde
www.sci-globe.de

Virtuelle Fachbibliotheken
www.virtuellefachbibliothek.de

Zeitschriftendatenbank
www.zeitschriftendatenbank.de

The Authors

The Translator

Jürgen Seefeldt, born in 1953, studied public librarianship in Cologne. Employment as Certified Librarian *(Dipo.-Bibliothekar)* at the City Library (Stadtbücherei) of Hamm, the Technical Library of the United Electricity Corporation of Westphalia *(Vereinigte Elektrizitätswerke Westfalen)* in Dortmund; from 1979 – 1985 deputy director of the City Library *(Stadtbücherei)* of Herne, from 1985-1991 Director of the Country Libraries *(Kreisbüchereien)* of Unna; since 1991 Director of State Service Center for Public Libraries *(Landesbüchereistelle)* Rheineland-Palatinate in Koblenz. Over the years, adjunct instructor at the University of Applied Sciences, Cologne (FH Köln) and the University of Applied Sciences for Public Librarianship of the *Borromäusvereins* in Bonn. From 1995 – 1998 co-editor of the professional journal *BuB*, from 1998 – 2001 member of the National Executive Director of the DBV-Regional Association for the Rhineland-Palatinate *(DBV-Landesverbandes Rheinland-Pfalz)*, Member of the Executive Board of the Conference of the State Service Centers for Public Libraries in Germany *(Fachkonferenz der Staatlichen Büchereistellen* in Deutschland). Author of numerous articles and book chapters. Co-author of the book "Seefeldt/Metz: Unterhaltungsliteratur in Öffentlichen Bibliotheken" and the 3rd edition of the handbook "Busse-Ernestus-Plassmann-Seefeldt: Das Bibliothekswesen in Deutschland".

Dr. Ludger Syré, born in 1953, studied history and German Language and Literature in Freiburg, Munich and Tübingen, with a doctorate in East European history; Training as Academic and Research Librarian *(Wissenschaftlicher Bibliothekar)* in Tübingen and Cologne; since 1987 subject specialist / reference librarian for history, collaborator for the State Bibliography *(Landesbibliographie)* of Baden-Württemberg and Head of the Technical Department of the State Library of Baden *(Badischen Landesbibliothek)* in Kalsruhe; Instructor at the Institute for History of the University of Karlsruhe; between 1992 and 2002 two years in the Executive Board and eight years in the Membership Committee of the Association of German Librarians *(Verein Deutscher Bibliothekare)* as well as seven years executive director of the State Association of the VDB for Baden-Württemberg *(VDB-Landesverbandes Baden-Württemberg)*; Author of numerous contributions to books and journals.

Dr. Diann Rusch-Feja studied education, English and American literature, German language and literature, and library science at various universities in the USA and Germany. She holds a B.S. in education (1973), an M.A.(1976), an M.L.S.(1981) and Ph.D. (1986), as well as a New York State Permanent Teacher's License. She was a Fulbright Scholar 1979-80. Her work experience includes 1983-84 Follow-up and Records Officer, British Council Headquarters, Cologne; 1984-1988 System Specialist, McDonnell-Douglas Information Systems; 1989-2002 Head Librarian, Max Planck Institute for Human Development, Berlin; and since 2002 Director, Information Resource Center, International University Bremen. She has taught various courses in library science since 1992, including 1998 Visiting Associate Professor, School of Information and Library Science, University of Wisconsin-Madison. Officer in: 1997-2002 Executive Board, DBV Regional Branch Berlin; 1998-2003 Advisory Board, German Special Libraries Association (ASpB), since 1997 Standing Committee of the IFLA Section on Information Technology (1998-2001 Secretary-Treasurer); since 2000 Steering Committee of the Open Archives Initiative; since 1996 Advisory Committee Dublin Core Metadata Initiative.

Subject Index
(Names, Institutions,
Abbreviations)